OCCASIONAL P

Economic Adjustment in Low-Income Countries

Experience Under the Enhanced Structural Adjustment Facility

Susan Schadler, Franek Rozwadowski,
Siddharth Tiwari, and David O. Robinson

INTERNATIONAL MONETARY FUND
Washington DC
September 1993

Cataloging-in-Publication Data

Economic adjustment in low-income countries : experience under the Enhanced Structural Adjustment Facility / Susan Schadler ... [et al.]. — Washington, D.C. : International Monetary Fund, [1993]
p. ; cm. — (Occasional paper ; ISSN 0251-6365 ; 106)

ISBN 1-55775-336-9

1. Structural adjustment (Economic policy) — Developing countries. 2. Loans, Foreign — Developing countries. 3. International Monetary Fund — Developing countries. 4. Sustainable development — Developing countries. I. Schadler, Susan. II. International Monetary Fund. III. Series : Occasional paper (International Monetary Fund) ; no. 106.
HC59.7.E253 1993

Price: US$15.00
(US$12.00 to full-time faculty members and students at universities and colleges)

Please send orders to:
International Monetary Fund, Publication Services
700 19th Street, N.W., Washington, D.C. 20431, U.S.A.
Tel.: (202) 623-7430 Telefax: (202) 623-7201

recycled paper

Contents

Boxes

Tables

Charts

Statistical Appendix Tables

The following symbols have been used throughout this paper:

... to indicate that data are not available;

— to indicate that the figure is zero or less than half the digit shown, or that the item does not exist;

– between years or months (e.g., 1991–92 or January–June) to indicate the years or months covered, including the beginning and ending years or months;

/ between years (e.g., 1991/92) to indicate a crop or fiscal (financial) year.

"Billion" means a thousand million.

Minor discrepancies between constituent figures and totals are due to rounding.

The term "country," as used in this paper, does not in all cases refer to a territorial entity that is a state as understood by international law and practice; the term also covers some territorial entities that are not states, but for which statistical data are maintained and provided internationally on a separate and independent basis.

Preface

This paper is based on a study that was conducted in late 1992 as part of the IMF's ongoing process of reviewing its lending facilities. It reflects information available at the end of 1992. The authors are indebted to numerous members of Fund area departments for detailed comments on the paper, to Kirsten Fitchett for research assistance, and to Olivia Carolin and Anna Vahdati for secretarial assistance. They wish to thank J. R. Morrison of the External Relations Department, who edited the manuscript and coordinated its publication.

The opinions expressed in the paper are those of the authors and do not necessarily reflect the views of the IMF or of its Executive Directors.

I Introduction

Following broadly satisfactory growth, inflation, and external performance during the 1960s and 1970s, many low-income countries encountered serious economic difficulties in the early 1980s. These problems frequently stemmed from a clash between stark reversals of the terms of trade and expansionary financial policies. Long-standing structural weaknesses placed countries in a poor position to adjust to their setbacks while sustaining growth. Often, the first response to the adverse developments was to borrow more, and by the mid-1980s, many low-income countries found themselves facing not only massive stabilization problems but also excessive external debt burdens.

In these circumstances, adjustment programs focusing on financial policies alone would not address the roots of countries' problems. Beyond changes in financial policies, major reforms in the structure and institutions of the economies—particularly in the role of the government and incentives for production—were needed. Moreover, the exceptionally heavy indebtedness of these countries required both debt-service relief and strict limits on new borrowing on nonconcessional terms—limits that precluded even borrowing from the IMF on conventional terms.

In 1986, the IMF responded to these needs by setting up the Structural Adjustment Facility (SAF), funded by proceeds from earlier sales of gold. This initiative was taken a step further with the establishment of the Enhanced Structural Adjustment Facility (ESAF) in 1987 (see Box 1), with financing derived in part from SAF resources and in part from contributions in the form of loans as well as grants administered by the ESAF Trust. The ESAF was designed to promote adjustment and reform in eligible countries by supporting particularly vigorous macroeconomic and structural change with a larger scale of resources on the same concessional terms as the SAF. The explicit objectives of the ESAF are to promote external viability and higher output in a balanced manner by reducing domestic and external imbalances, mobilizing resources, and improving resource allocation. Policy programs supported by ESAF resources are to aim at a substantial move, during the three-year program period, toward an overall external position and structure of the balance of payments consistent with orderly relations with

Box 1. The Structural Adjustment Facility (SAF) and the Enhanced Structural Adjustment Facility (ESAF)

The SAF was set up in March 1986 to provide highly concessional loans to support structural adjustment in low-income countries; the ESAF was set up in December 1987 to support especially vigorous adjustment programs with a higher level of access. Sixty-two low-income countries were eligible for access to the SAF and ESAF. In April 1992 eligibility was extended to a further 11 countries. As of end-July 1993, a total of 36 countries had had arrangements under the SAF and 29 countries under the ESAF.

Under both facilities adjustment is normally carried out in three successive annual programs (though the ESAF now provides for a fourth-year arrangement in exceptional circumstances). Each annual program forms the first year of a three-year policy framework elaborated in a policy framework paper (PFP). The PFPs are drawn up in a collaborative effort by the country authorities, the IMF, and the World Bank; they establish an agenda for mutually supporting macroeconomic adjustment and structural reforms and may be used to attract financial support from donors.

In line with the needs of low-income countries, financial support under the SAF and ESAF is on concessional terms—an interest rate of 0.5 percent to be repaid beginning five and a half years and ending ten years after disbursement. Cumulative access under the SAF over the three years of the arrangement is now fixed at 50 percent of the country's IMF quota; access under the ESAF is 110 percent of quota on average, although in exceptional circumstances a country may obtain up to 255 percent of quota over the three years of the arrangement.

creditors (including the IMF) and a trade and payments system free of restrictions.

The operational guidelines for ESAF-supported programs specified more detailed macroeconomic objectives in three areas.

- *Economic growth*. Programs were to create the conditions to achieve sustained economic growth at or near potential output and, indeed, to raise potential over time in a noninflationary manner. It was recognized, however, that in some countries, an increase in growth could not be expected during the program period.
- *Balance of payments*. Ideally, programs were to aim at attaining, by the end of the program period, an external current account deficit that could be financed by normal and sustainable capital inflows (including aid). When large initial debt burdens did not permit this, more limited goals were to be sought: any rescheduling after the program period would affect principal only; other forms of exceptional financing after the program period would be limited to grants and highly concessional loans; and new borrowing would be serviced on schedule. It was recognized that even these limited objectives might require debt reduction or high levels of exceptional financing on concessional terms during the program period.
- *Structural policies*. The staffs of the IMF and the World Bank were to cooperate with governments to identify and prioritize structural problems. ESAF programs were to focus on a few key problems that were within the expertise of the IMF and of greatest relevance to output and the balance of payments. The aim was to eliminate or substantially reduce these problems during the program period. Reforms were to be front-loaded whenever possible.

This paper examines the experience of 19 countries (see Chart 1) that had entered ESAF arrangements as of mid-1992 in order to determine the degree to which these three objectives were reached. This experience is examined by comparing recent developments with conditions prior to their SAF/ESAF period.[1] All but two of these countries had had at least a one-year program under the SAF prior to the ESAF arrangement; five countries had completed a full three-year ESAF period by mid-1992.[2] Because ESAF programs typically entailed a continuation and intensification of efforts begun in SAF programs, the review covers the experiences of countries under both SAF and ESAF programs.

The emphasis in this review is on taking stock of accomplishments under SAF- and ESAF-supported programs and on identifying areas where successor arrangements will need stronger efforts. Clear-cut conclusions on the reasons for differences in countries' performance have proved difficult to draw, except where those differences were stark. Thus, the experience of the few countries that undertook comprehensive and forceful adjustment suggests a strong correlation between improved economic performance and the strength of efforts to rein in financial policies and to shift processes for resource allocation from governments to markets. But when countries undertook adjustment in a more piecemeal and less vigorous fashion, explanations of differences in economic performance—such as the sequencing of policy changes—are not obvious. This opacity reflects two characteristics that muddy the assessment of even strong adjustment programs. First, countries faced diverse circumstances, so it was difficult to disentangle the effects of insufficiently comprehensive policy changes from those of adverse exogenous factors. Second, the strength of policy changes—particularly structural changes—was seldom quantifiable or comparable across countries.

The remainder of the review is organized in four sections. Section II describes the circumstances—both the initial conditions and the external environment—under which adjustment programs were formulated. Section III reviews the policy content of the SAF/ESAF programs. Section IV establishes criteria for gauging the success of SAF/ESAF arrangements both in terms of progress toward external viability and in terms of creating the conditions for sustained growth; it then uses them to measure progress under the SAF/ESAF arrangements. Concluding remarks are provided in Section V.

[1]The term "SAF/ESAF period" will be used to denote the period for each country starting with the program year of the first SAF- or ESAF-supported arrangement and ending with the most recent year for which data are available, 1991 or 1991/92.

[2]The remaining 14 countries either had initiated ESAF arrangements later in the period and were still implementing or negotiating annual ESAF programs or, in three cases, were experiencing delays in negotiating an annual program.

Chart 1. Annual Arrangements Under the SAF and ESAF[1]

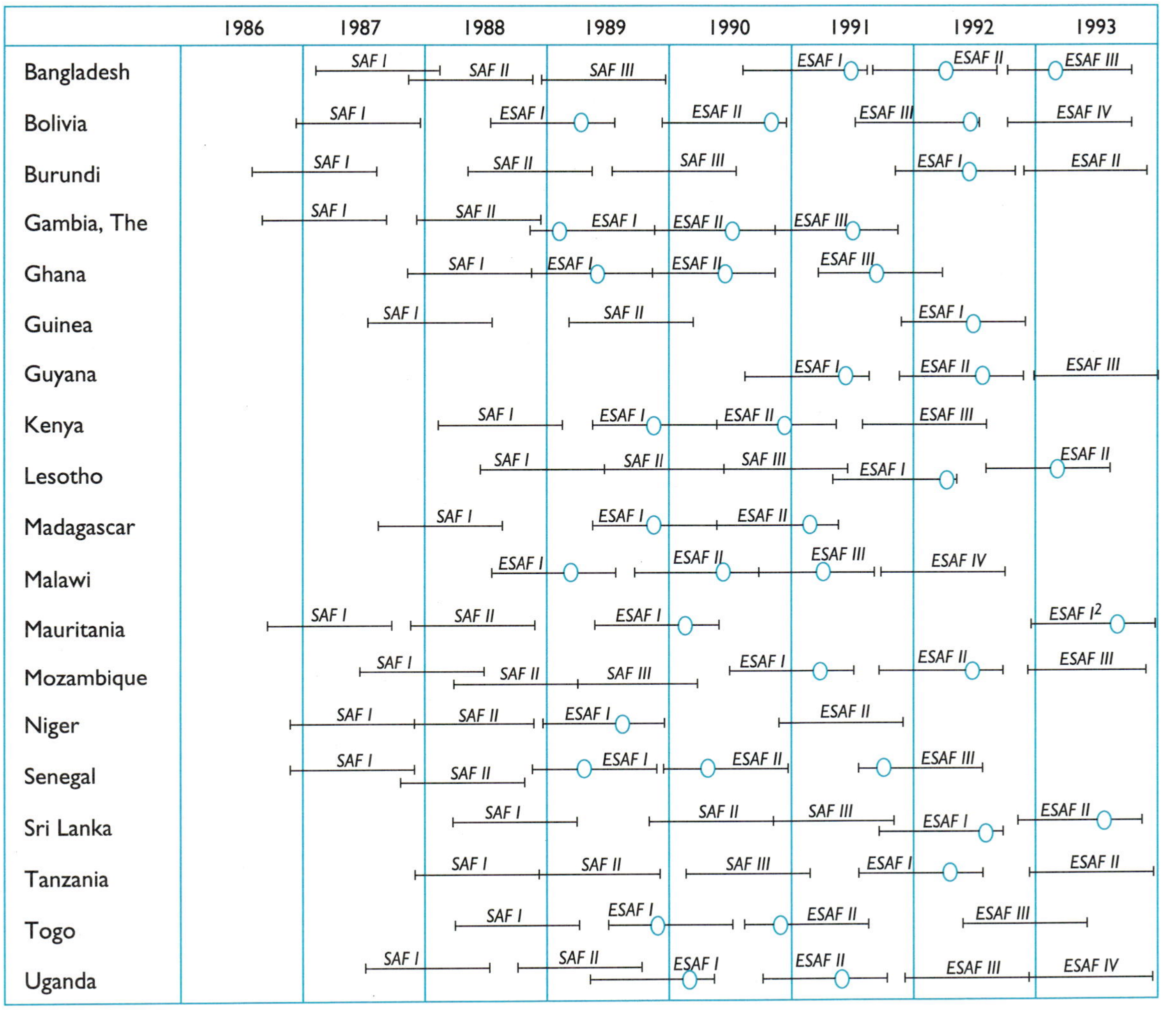

[1]Countries for which an ESAF arrangement was approved between 1988 and June 1992. Circles in the ESAF lines indicate dates when reviews were completed. The chart includes arrangements approved and reviews completed before end-July 1993.

[2]New ESAF arrangement after the eligibility period of first three-year ESAF arrangement had expired.

II The Setting

The economic and social structures of the 19 countries under review made them unusually vulnerable to adverse weather and world market conditions as well as poor domestic financial policies. Incomes per capita were among the lowest in the world; population growth rates were among the highest in the world; agriculture typically accounted for one-third, but in some countries as much as two-thirds, of measured GDP; exports tended to be concentrated in a few primary commodities; and almost all energy needs were met through imports. Most countries had elaborate networks of state intervention—price controls, government-run distribution systems, and public ownership of strategic industries—ostensibly to alleviate the fragility of their productive bases. In practice, however, the public sector's dominance in the economy added to inherent weaknesses by rendering the supply side of the economy inefficient and unresponsive to market signals.

Initial Conditions

By the mid-1980s the interplay among the weak productive bases, periodic disruptions from poor weather or civil strife, sharp deteriorations in the terms of trade, and inadequate policy responses to emerging problems had left most of the countries with low growth and large external imbalances (Chart 2 and Appendix Table A1). In all but five countries, real GDP per capita had fallen during the three or more years preceding the first SAF or ESAF arrangement. Often, the most pronounced weakness was in the export sector. Absorption, however, was kept high by large public sector deficits financed by bank credit and external inflows.

This situation gave rise to economic pressures. External current account deficits, large throughout the 1980s, had averaged 12 percent of GDP during the three years preceding the first SAF/ESAF arrangement for the group as a whole. This large financing requirement resulted in a rapid increase in external debt, to levels that were for most countries clearly unmanageable. Thus, by the beginning of the SAF/ESAF period, 13 of the countries under review were unable to meet their debt-service obligations and resorted to reschedulings and arrears. Inflation rose—in five countries to more than 30 percent a year during the three years prior to the SAF/ESAF period. In the absence of fundamental policy adjustments, restrictions were placed on external trade and payments. Prospects for the medium term were compromised by savings rates that, at about 8 percent of GDP, were too low to support per capita income growth. The following paragraphs review the policy issues underlying these developments.

Fiscal Affairs

In each of the countries, large public sector deficits were believed to be the principal cause of the excess of absorption over output. However, data on consolidated public sector finances existed only for Bolivia and Guyana, so in other countries targets for the public sector had to be set without a quantified understanding of the size of the initial problem. More important, without data on financial flows between various levels of the public sector (central government, local governments, and public enterprises, including marketing boards), the origin of public sector imbalances was sometimes unclear. This uncertainty hindered the proper targeting of policies and the ability to assess their implementation and effectiveness.

Most of the countries entered the SAF/ESAF period with a history of large central government deficits (Chart 3). The median deficit (including grants) for the three years preceding the SAF/ESAF period was 6 percent of GDP; only Ghana, Madagascar, and Senegal had deficits smaller than 4 percent of GDP (Appendix Table A2). Two-thirds of the countries had made some progress in reducing fiscal deficits relative to GDP during the three years prior to the SAF/ESAF period—several by more than 2 percentage points and Bolivia, Burundi, and The Gambia by more than 5 percentage points.

Tax systems were nearly all narrowly based. Most

Chart 2. Growth, Inflation, and Current Account Prior to SAF/ESAF Period[1]
(Annual average for the three preceding years; in percent)

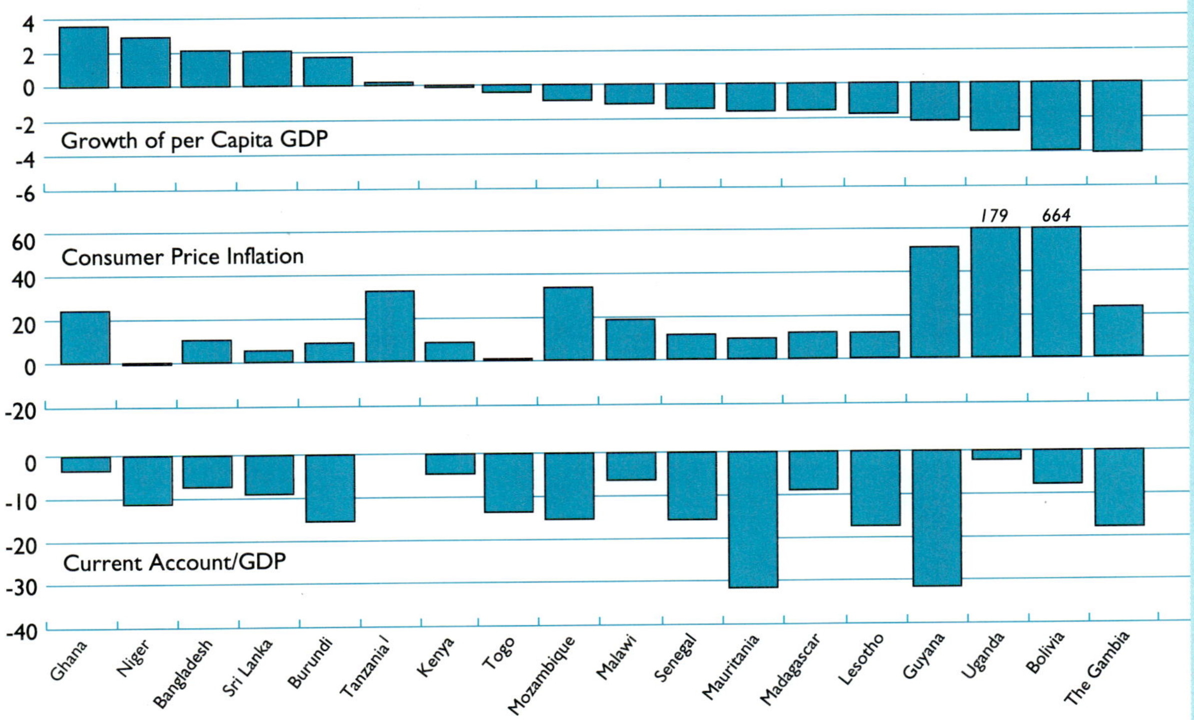

Sources: International Monetary Fund, *International Financial Statistics* (Washington), various issues; and IMF staff estimates.
[1]Data not available for Guinea or for Tanzania's current account to GDP ratio.

countries in the group were heavily dependent on a single source of revenue—often, specific taxes on international trade—with many exemptions, especially to public enterprises. Only six countries entered the SAF/ESAF period with a significant generalized sales tax. Administration was a major problem. These characteristics resulted in serious distortions and generally low elasticities.

Expenditure control was weak in most of the countries, usually reflecting inadequate monitoring or institutional weaknesses. As an extension of this problem, capital and current budgets were poorly integrated, giving rise to inadequate expenditure on maintenance and to levels of public investment that ranged widely: public investment during the three years prior to the SAF/ESAF period varied from less than 4 percent of GDP in three countries to more than 10 percent in another six. In most countries, transfers to public enterprises (either explicitly through cash payments and tax exemptions or implicitly through tax arrears and loan defaults) and excessive wage bills (stemming mainly from excessive employment) were a major burden on the budget.

State Intervention and Control

Public enterprises played an important role in production and employment in each of the countries under review. Such enterprises were typically concentrated in mining, manufacturing, and utilities. In addition, publicly owned marketing boards and trading monopolies for agricultural products and imports provided such services as transportation, marketing, price stabilization, credit provision, and processing (Appendix Table A3). For most countries, however, there are not systematic data on the role of public enterprises or on financial flows between public enterprises and the central government. It is, therefore, impossible to quantify the contribution of public enterprises to the overall public sector deficit, domestic activity, or employment. Sketchy data that are available suggest that many public enterprises operated with significant losses, earned low returns

Chart 3. Fiscal Conditions Prior to SAF/ESAF Period
(Annual average for the three preceding years; in percent of GDP)

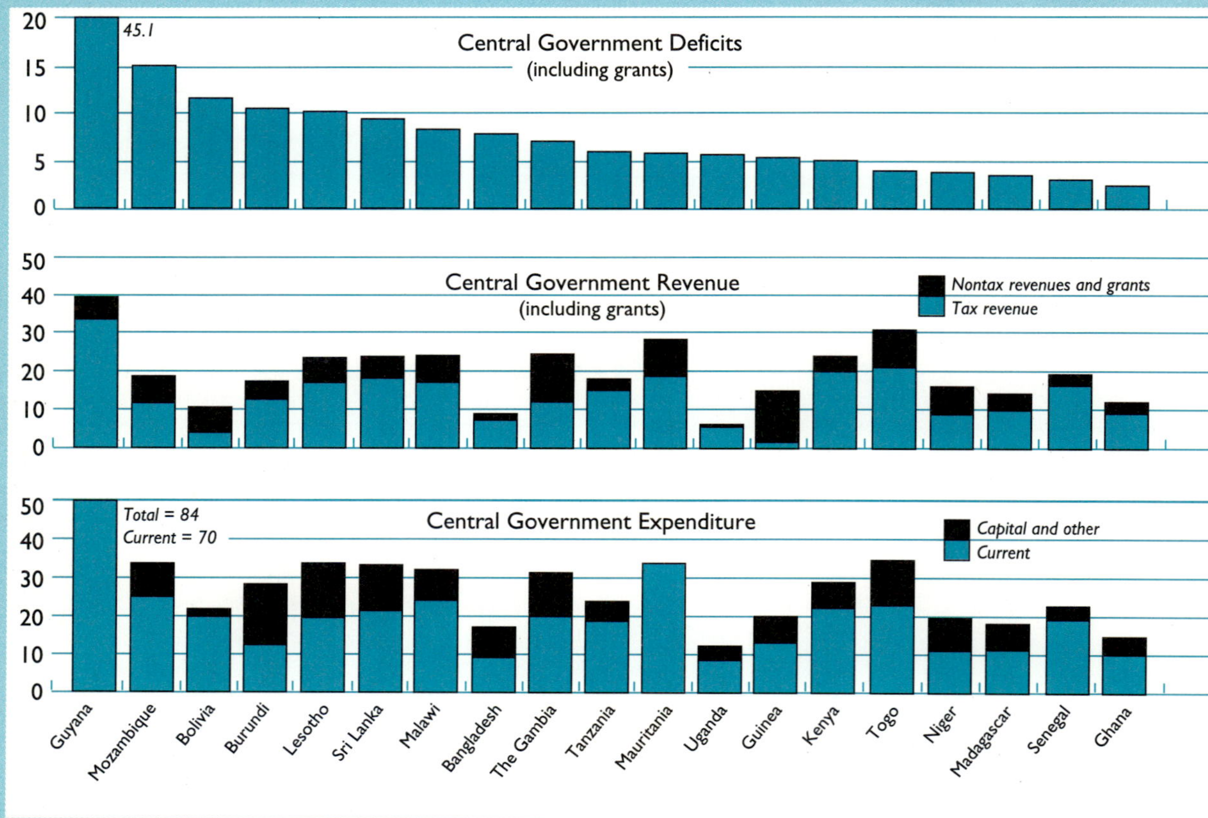

on investments, or were unable to generate resources for adequate investment.

Official control over prices was prevalent, but the extent varied widely—from comprehensive controls in Mozambique and Tanzania to a virtual absence of control in Lesotho and Bolivia (Appendix Table A3). Typically, prices of many strategic items were administered by state trading monopolies, marketing boards, or public enterprises. Affected prices included producer prices of agricultural exports, domestic prices of key imports (fertilizer, petroleum products, foodstuffs), and producer and consumer prices of domestically produced food grains. The distortionary impact of price controls depended on whether they were designed to subsidize production or consumption, shield domestic producers or consumers from fluctuations in international prices, or raise revenue. In many countries, agriculture was promoted by subsidizing imported fertilizer or paying high producer prices. In other countries, producer prices were kept low in order to generate revenues for the marketing boards or subsidize consumption.

A number of the countries under review maintained overvalued currencies supported by restrictive exchange and trade systems. The degree of exchange control prior to countries' first SAF- or ESAF-supported programs varied enormously (Appendix Table A4). In six countries where the exchange rate was broadly fixed, comprehensive foreign exchange controls were administered through the centralized allocation of surrendered export receipts, and parallel market premia were typically in excess of 100 percent. Another six countries were essentially free of restrictions on current transactions. Four of these (Lesotho, Niger, Senegal, and Togo) maintained fixed exchange rates in the context of currency unions; in the other two (Bolivia and The Gambia), exchange rates were determined in recently established auctions or interbank markets. The remaining seven countries had partial controls exercised through various institutional structures including secondary exchange markets and foreign exchange retention schemes.

In all but 5 of the 19 countries, aggressive nominal depreciations had resulted in real depreciations over the three years leading up to the SAF/ESAF period, in spite of high inflation rates.[3] In addition to Burundi, exceptions were Mozambique and Uganda (where high inflation had produced large real appreciations) and Senegal and Togo (where the strength of the French franc combined with expansionary domestic policies had appreciated the real effective exchange rate).

In most of the 19 countries the state exercised tight control over interest rates and the allocation of credit. Interest rates were either administered directly or controlled through floors and ceilings or limits on spreads. Real interest rates (nominal rates less contemporaneous inflation) were negative in eight countries, mostly those with high inflation and inflexible nominal interest rates (Appendix Table A2); in contrast, countries with low inflation and more flexible nominal interest rates often had positive real interest rates. Most countries allocated credit through quantitative ceilings imposed by bank or by sector. Because these policies tended to accommodate the deficits of the public enterprises, nonperforming loans were significant. This situation, together with poor incentives for depositors, frequently resulted in bank insolvencies.

The design and implementation of reforms in each of these areas was frequently impeded by weak administrative capacity, although countries varied widely in this regard. For example, in Bolivia, consolidated accounts for the nonfinancial public sector were available, whereas in Guinea there was not even a monetary survey. The most serious problems were in the capacity to formulate and monitor the government budget, administer tax collection, and manage externally funded public investment projects. Weak administrative capacity sometimes stemmed from a large, but inefficient and unmotivated, civil service.

Previous Reform Efforts

Most of the 19 countries had begun the process of reform and macroeconomic stabilization—often with IMF support—prior to their SAF/ESAF arrangements. Typically, previous programs had included reductions in financial imbalances and adjustments to prices and exchange rates. In several countries—Bolivia, The Gambia, Ghana, Guyana, and Niger—significant reform efforts were under way at the inception of the first SAF or ESAF arrangements. The SAF/ESAF arrangements were therefore designed to sustain and extend the reform. In several other countries, promising reform efforts had stalled (Guinea, Kenya, Mauritania, and Sri Lanka). Some countries (Lesotho and Mozambique) were undertaking IMF-supported reforms for the first time.

External and Domestic Environment During SAF/ESAF Arrangements

The external environment during the SAF/ESAF period presented both adverse and positive influences. On the negative side, growth in the major industrial countries slowed, particularly from 1990 on. This slowdown, together with commodity-specific developments, resulted in deteriorating terms of trade for most of the ESAF countries—on average for the group as a whole by 5 percent a year. There was, however, considerable diversity across the 19 countries (Chart 4 and Appendix Tables A5, A6). In Bangladesh, Malawi, and Senegal, the terms of trade actually improved during their SAF/ESAF arrangements, while at the other extreme, in Uganda and Madagascar, the average annual decline during the arrangements exceeded 10 percent. In almost half of the countries, declines in export prices were an important component of the weakening terms of trade. This trend strained the process of making conditions for exporters more responsive to world prices—an important focus in most SAF- and ESAF-supported programs.

On the positive side, net resource transfers from the rest of the world rose sharply, and new borrowing was on increasingly concessional terms. Not only were resources secured through consultative/support groups and bilateral contacts, but new undertakings (like the World Bank's Special Program of Assistance for Debt Distressed Countries in Sub-Saharan Africa) added to the support. Thus, for the countries as a group, the net resource transfer increased by 60 percent during the SAF/ESAF period to more than US$6 billion in 1991 (Appendix Table A7). Grants, which rose by two-thirds, constituted the bulk of this increase. There was a wide range across countries both in the size of and changes in net resource transfers. In the most recent year, the transfer was about 1 percent of GDP in Kenya and slightly over 50 percent of GDP in Mozambique; this represented a slight drop relative to the pre-SAF period in Kenya but an increase relative to GDP of almost 40 percentage points in Mozambique.

Before the ESAF programs, Paris Club creditors had responded flexibly to the need for cash flow

[3]In half of the countries, the real depreciation exceeded 10 percent.

Chart 4. External Developments During SAF/ESAF Period

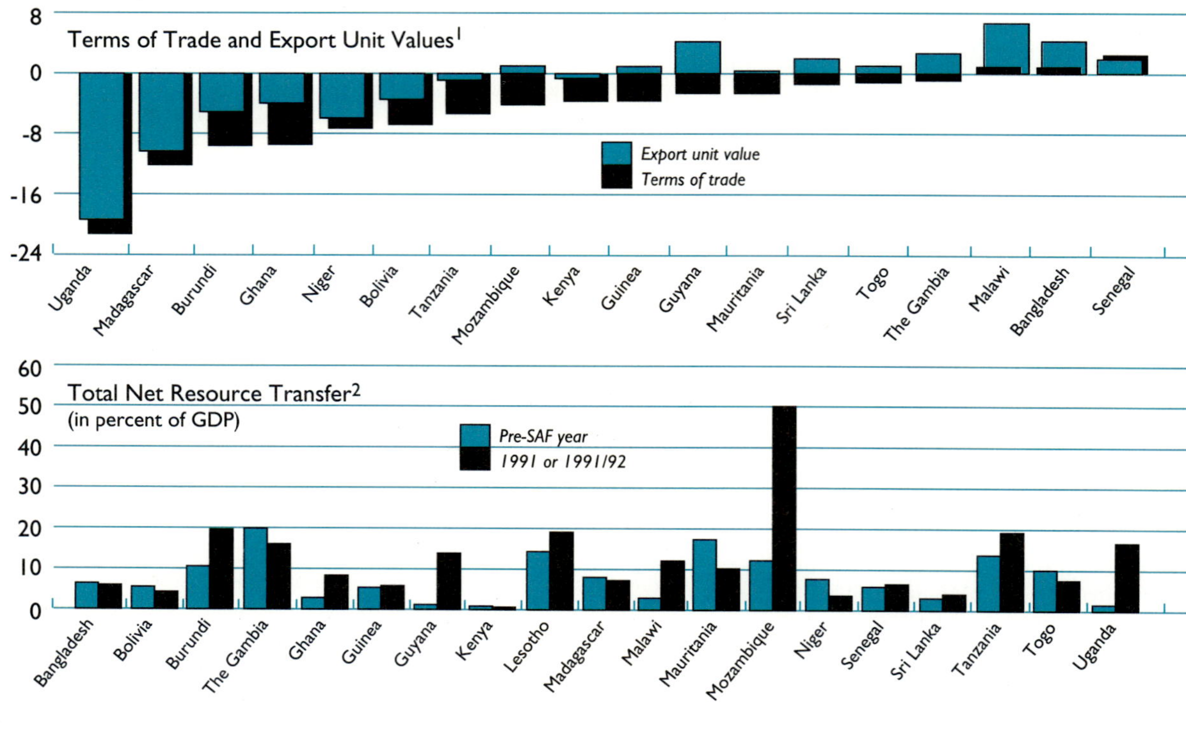

Sources: Statistical Appendix Tables A5 and A7.
[1]Average annual percent change between the first year of the SAF/ESAF arrangement and 1991.
[2]Defined as all official loans and grants plus net IMF purchases less actual debt-service payments made.

relief on existing debts of countries that adopted IMF-supported programs. They also safeguarded the flow of new external financing to rescheduling countries. In response to the protracted problems of the heavily indebted countries, however, Paris Club creditors introduced in late 1988 a menu of options (the "Toronto terms") including partial cancellation, extensions of maturities, and concessions on interest rates. Eleven of the countries rescheduled their debt under Toronto terms options (Appendix Table A8).

By the early 1990s, it was recognized that even with sustained adjustment efforts, greater concessions would be needed if debt burdens in the low-income countries were to become manageable. Enhanced concessions were incorporated into Paris Club reschedulings beginning in December 1991. This new menu provided for a 50 percent reduction (in net present value terms) of debt-service payments consolidated on non-ODA (Official Development Assistance) debts through either an outright cancellation of 50 percent of the consolidated claims or a rescheduling at concessional interest rates. The menu also included the nonconcessional options available under Toronto terms. Creditors agreed to provide an effective debt reduction of the same order of magnitude on concessional loans. The agreements also provided for creditors' reexamining whether to cancel part of the remaining stock of debt after a few years, if previous reschedulings were fully implemented, other nonmultilateral creditors granted comparable relief, and appropriate arrangements with the IMF were continued. As of the end of 1992, 5 of the 19 ESAF countries had availed themselves of the enhanced concessions. Creditors have also provided debt relief to several of the ESAF countries outside the Paris Club.

Several countries faced adverse domestic conditions during their SAF/ESAF period. Civil unrest created serious economic disruptions in Madagascar, Mozambique, Sri Lanka, and Togo. In Southern Africa, a drought beginning in 1990 took a large toll on agricultural output and exports.

III Financial and Structural Policies: The Broad Front for Reform

The exceptionally weak economic performance and structural characteristics of the ESAF countries meant that a wide range of policy changes and reforms were needed. Generally, programs aimed at containing excess demand as well as addressing structural weakness, although in most countries the need for stabilization was not as dire as in many IMF-supported adjustment programs in Latin America and Eastern Europe. For most of the countries under review, the strategy underlying the structural reform program was to strengthen the financial position of the public sector and to reduce the government's interference in the allocation of resources.

Typically, the reforms needed were closely interrelated. For example, in many countries reform of public enterprises and marketing boards was essential to reducing subsidies, strengthening the tax base, and addressing, in a lasting manner, weaknesses in the banking system. In turn, when currencies were overvalued, reforms in marketing boards and price controls required exchange rate adjustments if incentives to exporters were to be improved or maintained. Depreciations, however, could not be sustained in real terms without fiscal adjustment. Since there was no obvious place to break into this circle from initial positions that were typically highly distressed, the approach taken was generally as broad-based as possible.

In practice, the aggressiveness with which policies were implemented varied. In broad qualitative terms, there appears to have been more progress with reforms to exchange and trade systems, price controls, and marketing boards than in restructuring public enterprises or addressing weaknesses in the financial system. In most countries, central government deficits were reduced but often without the needed broad-based tax and expenditure reforms. Although the reasons for the differing success and pace of reforms were varied, a few general themes emerge from this review. First, the political commitment to reform was critical; in light of the history in most of these countries of centralized control and government ownership of productive activities, such commitment often required a break with deeply rooted views about the political economy. Second, vested interests often aligned themselves against reforms, and ways to soften the blow to these groups and persuade them of the longer term benefits of reform were important. Third, deteriorating terms of trade often impeded reform initiatives, both because they masked the benefits of reform, thereby eroding political support, and because they presented an urgent adjustment problem of their own. Fourth, administrative capacity was exceptionally weak, and many delays reflected inappropriate initial expectations of how quickly the technical expertise could be developed to design, implement, and sustain the reforms.

In this latter connection the IMF, the World Bank, and many other bilateral and multilateral agencies offered extensive technical assistance. The IMF's particular contributions were concentrated in the areas of tax design and administration, central government budget formulation and expenditure control, financial sector reform (particularly the development of indirect means of monetary control, securities and money markets, and interest rate liberalization), and exchange system reform. The IMF also provided technical assistance to help in the development of statistics, especially in the areas of monetary accounts, balance of payments, and national accounts—areas where data deficiencies severely impeded the identification of policy problems and the monitoring of programs addressing them.

All SAF/ESAF arrangements were the outcome of strengthened collaboration among the country authorities, the World Bank, and the IMF under the umbrella of a policy framework paper (PFP) (see Box 1). Typically, different parts of the adjustment program were supported by regional development banks and bilateral donors, and it is rarely possible to segregate the effects of SAF/ESAF arrangements from the effects of International Development Association (IDA) and other credits. Nevertheless, it is clear that the PFP mechanism has enhanced the coordination of the IMF's support for macroeconomic adjustment and structural reforms with the World Bank's support for structural reforms in diverse areas such as trade, taxation, financial intermediation, public enterprises, public expenditure and investment, agricultural marketing, and the social dimensions of adjustment.

Public Sector Policies

Reforms of the public sector were typically geared toward strengthening its financial position and narrowing its focus to activities that the private sector could not perform efficiently. Frequently, however, the first of these objectives was hindered by the lack of consolidated public sector accounts that would identify the source of financial imbalance within the public sector. There were, however, indications in most countries that financial weaknesses permeated the various levels of the public sector. Consequently, reforms were targeted at all levels except, in most countries, local governments. Often, local government activity appeared minor relative to other segments of the public sector and, in any case, largely out of the control of the central government.

Central Government

Measuring the strength of adjustment of a central government is not as straightforward as it might seem. The improvement in a government's financial position is, of course, one readily available indicator. But in SAF/ESAF programs, structural changes in the areas of taxation and the controlling and prioritizing of expenditures were often as important as improving the financial position itself; yet, these changes did not always produce immediate positive results. Even when they did, such results were sometimes masked by the effects of adverse weather or changes in the terms of trade or other exogenous influences on revenues and expenditures.

Nevertheless, the imperative of stabilizing the economy meant that each of the countries did target an improvement in the broadest measure of the central government's net financial influence on the economy—the deficit including official grants. In a few countries, however, where sizable reductions in the deficit had occurred in the three years prior to the SAF/ESAF period, the targeted additional improvements were very small. In fact, the government's financial position including grants did improve in 13 of the 19 countries (Chart 5 and Appendix Table A9). In three of these countries—Guyana, Lesotho, and Mozambique—the cumulative improvement relative to GDP was more than 9 percentage points; although the deficits of these countries, except Lesotho, remained large, the reduction represented a distinct break from recent experience. For the other ten countries, the reduction in the deficit relative to GDP was more modest: on average the cumulative change over the average five years of their SAF/ESAF arrangements was about 2 percentage points of GDP compared with an average pre-SAF deficit of about 6 percent of GDP.[4] For the six countries that experienced a deterioration in their fiscal position, the decline amounted to about 1½ percentage points over a cumulative average five-year period, compared with an average pre-SAF deficit of about 4 percent of GDP.

While the central government deficit including grants is the best statement of a government's financial impact on the economy, the adjustment effort—to the extent that it can be captured in a financial balance—is better reflected in the government's primary current account excluding grants.[5] The directions of the changes in primary current accounts largely matched those of the overall balances (Chart 5 and Appendix Table A9). Typically, however, the primary current account improved less or deteriorated more than the overall balance. This reflects the fact that, on average, scheduled interest payments fell during the SAF/ESAF period, while grants rose by slightly more than capital spending: these two factors together accounted for about 40 percent of the improvement in the overall balance of the central government including grants in the 13 countries where an improvement occurred. The drop in interest payments resulted from declines in domestic interest rates, as inflation in some countries fell, and from lower scheduled interest payments on foreign debt in countries where the exchange rate was stable.

Increases in revenues generally accounted for most of the reduction in primary current account deficits (Chart 6).[6] These increases mostly stemmed from higher tax receipts and often reflected two main influences: first, during the early stages of the SAF/ESAF period, policy changes that eliminated the parallel market and thereby increased the share of economic activity in the tax net; and second, structural reforms to the tax system. Most countries undertook some tax policy measures to broaden the tax base and improve tax administration, but only in a few countries were these changes part of more comprehensive reforms. Mozambique stands out as

[4]Provisional outcomes for 1992 or 1992/93 suggest a weakening in fiscal performance in some of these countries. These results reflect slippages in policies but also such exogenous developments as the drought in Southern Africa.

[5]The primary current account excludes interest payments, which are beyond the control of present policies, and capital transactions, both expenditures and receipts, which tend to be driven by the availability of foreign grants.

[6]The exception was Guyana, where a significant part of the adjustment came from the expenditure side.

Chart 5. Central Government Financial Profiles
(In percent of GDP)

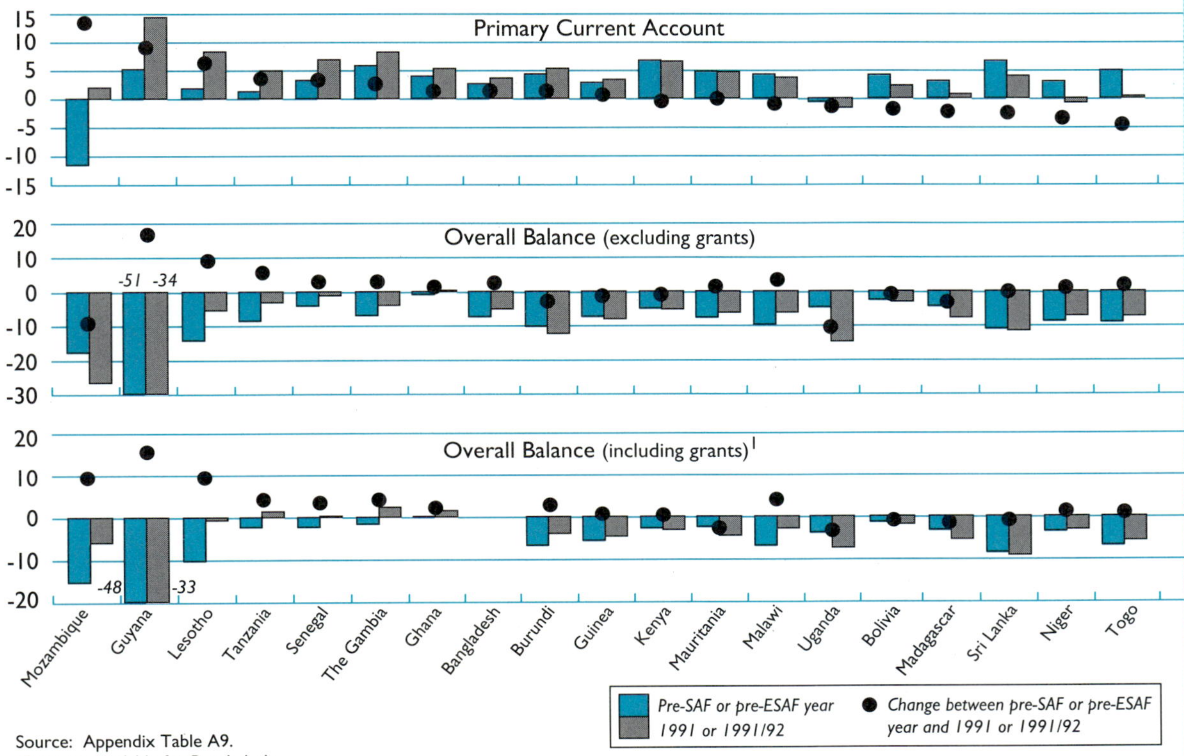

Source: Appendix Table A9.
[1]Data not available for Bangladesh.

an exception; sweeping changes in the tax system and a strengthening of tax administration contributed to a doubling of tax revenues relative to GDP. Other significant measures were the introduction of value-added taxes in six countries—Bangladesh, Bolivia, Kenya, Malawi, Niger, and Senegal—mostly just prior to or early in the program period.

Most of the countries that suffered sharp reductions in their terms of trade owing to falling export prices—Bolivia, Burundi, Ghana, Madagascar, Niger, and Uganda—were reasonably successful at insulating revenues. Although receipts from export-related taxes fell sharply in these countries, total revenues generally rose slightly relative to GDP. The two exceptions were Madagascar and Niger, where political disturbances contributed to a breakdown in tax administration, and revenues dropped to less than 10 percent of GDP. In some countries, the effect of the drop in export prices was cushioned by exchange rate changes, which lessened the impact on the export tax receipts and raised receipts from ad valorem import taxes. Generally, however, these countries had to act aggressively through other tax measures to compensate for the loss of export-related tax receipts. Even though these efforts succeeded in preventing a fall in revenues relative to GDP, overall fiscal deficits usually exceeded targets.

Current, noninterest expenditure was restrained in most countries; spending relative to GDP declined in more than half the countries, and there was a large absolute reduction in Guyana (Chart 7). For most countries, efforts to restrain expenditure focused on subsidies and civil service wage bills. The scope for reducing subsidies was closely tied to reform of public enterprises, marketing boards, and price controls, which are discussed later in this section. The net effect of these reforms is not transparent, however, because subsidization often took such indirect forms as tax exemptions or preferential

Chart 6. Central Government Revenue and Grants
(In percent of GDP)

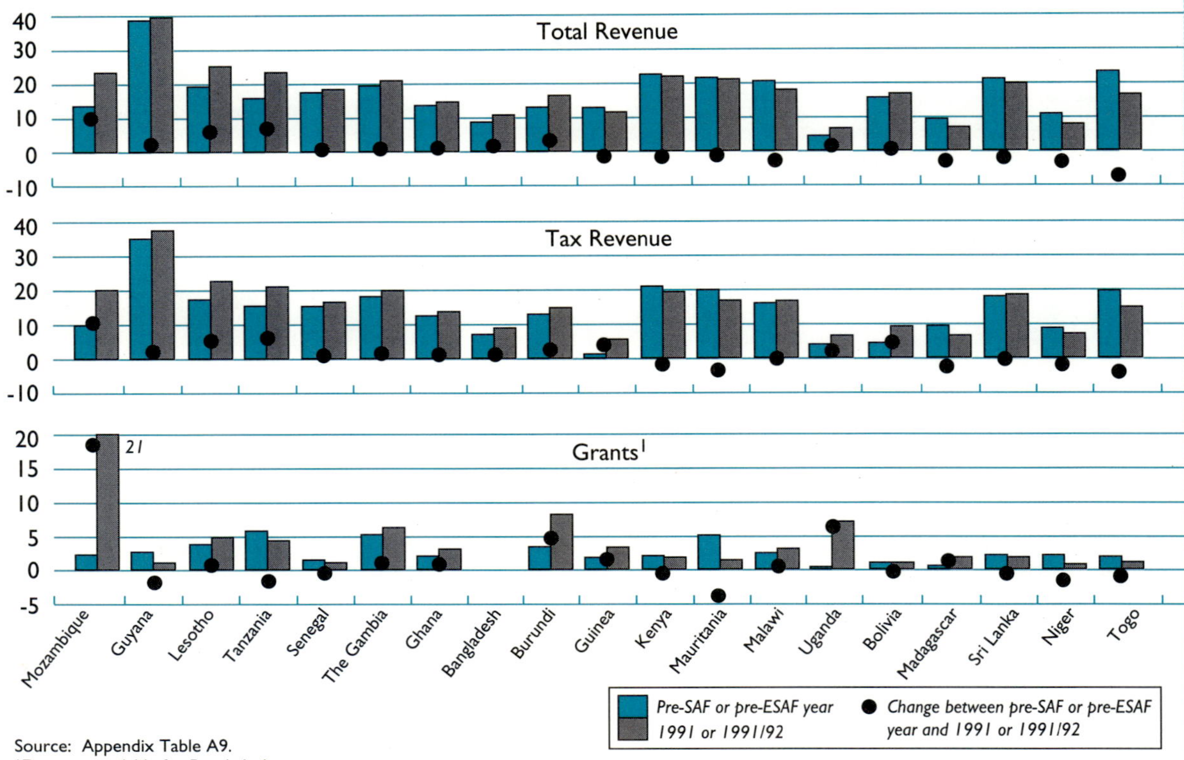

Source: Appendix Table A9.
[1]Data not available for Bangladesh.

credit for public sector entities or portions of the private sector. Civil service reform of varying degrees took place in 13 countries. The reforms focused on creating a smaller but more productive civil service by eliminating ghost workers and redundant tasks. As a first step, many countries undertook a civil service census to assess the magnitude of the problem. A few countries then proceeded to alter salary structures to attract or retain experienced staff. Several countries froze recruitment or actually reduced staff. However, the scope for action on the civil service was constrained in some countries by large increases in capital expenditures, which generated additional recurrent staffing requirements for maintenance.

In most ESAF countries, comprehensive public expenditure reviews were needed to guide fiscal consolidation and to increase the efficiency of public spending—both recurrent and capital. In almost all countries, efforts were made to improve the prioritization and monitoring of government outlays. For recurrent expenditures, systems for classifying and reconciling accounts between the Treasury, other government accounts, and the central bank were improved. For capital expenditures, rolling public investment programs or reviews of public investment were typically carried out by the World Bank. The implementation of these programs and recommendations was frequently part of the macroeconomic conditionality of IDA credits. These efforts have met with varying degrees of effectiveness and need to remain an important focus for future programs.

Rehabilitating and extending infrastructure was begun under the SAF/ESAF arrangements in several countries. In Guyana, Mozambique, and Uganda—where negligence, war, or forces of nature had destroyed much of the infrastructure—a vigorous effort to rebuild and rehabilitate was started. Capital expenditures (relative to GDP) increased in 10 of the 19 countries but, on average, remained broadly unchanged. Excluding Mozambique and Uganda, the

Chart 7. Central Government Expenditures
(In percent of GDP)

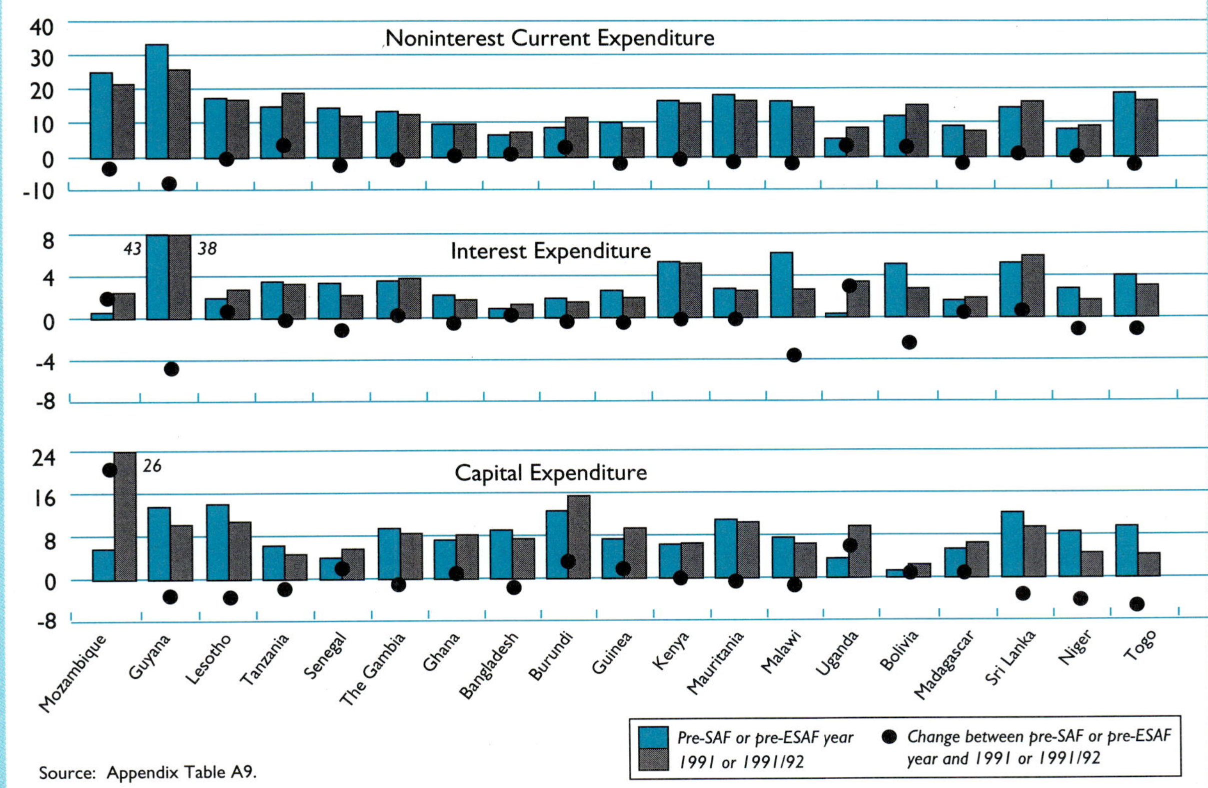

Source: Appendix Table A9.

average declined by nearly 1 percentage point of GDP. Declines often resulted from poor implementation capacity, delays in meeting conditions for donor financing, difficulties in mobilizing counterpart funds, and in a few countries, the cutting of capital expenditures to meet deficit reduction targets.

Nonfinancial Public Enterprises

Each of the SAF/ESAF-supported programs included a commitment to at least initiate public enterprise reform. Reform typically involved three stages: first, preparing studies to identify problems and propose solutions; second, implementing temporary measures to address the most egregious problems while legal changes for more far-reaching reforms were enacted; and third, carrying out fundamental reforms. A variety of such reforms were envisaged: enterprises considered strategically important were to be restructured or subjected to conditions approximating commercial standards; nonstrategic loss-making enterprises were to be liquidated; and nonstrategic enterprises with commercial value were to be privatized.

All these reforms encountered obstacles. Frequently, political commitment was lacking. In most of the countries under review, the public enterprise system embodied an economic ideology in which the state was to spearhead development in large part through its ownership of major enterprises. Recognition of the drawbacks of this strategy has only recently taken hold in some countries and is yet to come in others. Further important factors constraining progress were fears of output and employment losses; practical problems such as political unrest and the need to pace privatizations so as to avoid compromising the market value of enterprises to be sold and to develop some form of social safety net to protect redundant workers; and the lack of administrative capacity to implement reforms even when a plan for action did exist. In retrospect, the World Bank and IMF staff, as well as the authorities, have tended to underestimate the time required to design and implement reforms.

Only a few countries—Bolivia, The Gambia, Guyana, Senegal, Sri Lanka, and Togo—made significant inroads into the problem of public enterprises. While enterprise reform could not be considered complete in any of these countries, each did formulate a comprehensive reform program, enact needed legal changes, and implement parts of the program. With the exception of Guyana, these countries had seriously attempted—although usually in a halting fashion—to address problems in the public enterprise sector prior to the SAF/ESAF period. They therefore had formulated an agenda for reform even if some refinements for the SAF/ESAF period were needed. Also, except in Bolivia, legal changes required to proceed were not major. The substantive policies implemented in these countries took two main forms:

- *Restructuring* (principally to improve management and reduce workforces), usually reinforced by "performance contracts" between enterprises and the government that established commercial standards for enterprises. Guyana took a different route in employing management contracts with foreign companies to strengthen the operations of several major enterprises.
- *Divestiture*, although often of relatively small enterprises, or ones that did not constitute the heart of the problem in the enterprise sector. Exceptions were Guyana, where divestment was extensive, and Sri Lanka, where a large retrenchment of the labor force took place. Enterprise liquidation on a significant scale occurred only in Guyana, Senegal, and Togo.

Indicators of the financial performance of the enterprise sector are generally inadequate; in Guyana and Bolivia, where data do exist, performance appears to have improved markedly. Nevertheless, public enterprise reform in most of these countries is far from complete. In general, these countries need further divestiture and liquidation as well as a better definition of financial standards for enterprises that will remain under public ownership. Improving the data on the financial position of the enterprise sector will also be critical to monitoring the success of these efforts.

The other countries under review have not proceeded far in addressing the problems of public enterprises. A few—Burundi, Guinea, Malawi, Mauritania, Mozambique, and Niger—made progress in formulating plans to restructure or privatize some enterprises and in securing necessary legal changes. Others either did not have an articulated plan for reform or spent much of the SAF/ESAF period preparing such a plan. By and large, public enterprises remained a significant burden on the government budget for these countries, and any improvements in the financial position of enterprises tended to result from increases in their administered prices.

Marketing Boards and Trading Companies

For many countries, the most important reforms of the marketing system affected marketing boards for export commodities.[7] These reforms, in which support from the World Bank played an important role, generally had three aims: (1) to eliminate the monopoly of publicly owned marketing boards in the purchase, transportation, processing, and marketing of export commodities; (2) to allow market forces to determine producer prices; and (3) when marketing boards were not abolished, to improve their financial profiles. Similar objectives for reform applied to trading companies for domestically consumed goods (imported and domestically produced). Reforms of marketing boards and trading companies were one leg of the general effort to place greater reliance on markets to guide production and consumption—the other two were decontrolling prices and liberalizing exchange and trade restrictions.

Often, reforms to marketing boards were contingent on large exchange rate adjustments and changes in the exchange system. This was true for two common situations. In the first, marketing boards' losses were due largely to their attempts to counter the effects of an overvalued domestic currency by setting domestic producer prices above the official domestic currency value of world market prices. If export volumes were to be preserved while the financial position of marketing boards was strengthened, a depreciation, often with higher foreign exchange retention rates for producers, was essential. A second common situation was one in which producer prices had been held below the domestic currency value of world market prices, thus bolstering the financial positions of frequently inefficient marketing boards. Except when large savings could be generated by eliminating marketing boards or improving their efficiency, depreciations were also needed to raise returns to producers without sacrificing the financial position of the marketing boards.

Several countries—The Gambia, Guyana, Niger, and Uganda—came close to completing comprehensive reforms of their export marketing boards, although in Niger the problem was of a relatively small magnitude. The pattern of reform was similar

[7]In several countries—Bolivia, Guinea, Lesotho, and Sri Lanka—either marketing boards did not exist or problems had been addressed prior to the SAF/ESAF arrangements.

in these countries: a step devaluation (except in Niger, where exchange rate action is precluded by its membership in the West African Monetary Union, or WAMU) that permitted an attractive level of producer prices to be established while the financial position of the marketing boards was improved; the elimination of guaranteed minimum producer or support prices; permission for private participation in activities previously monopolized by marketing boards; and the termination of subsidies on agricultural inputs. As a result of such reforms, most producer prices in these countries are now either freely determined in markets or set by marketing boards on the basis of world prices they receive. Generally, marketing boards have been stripped of activities that could be performed more efficiently by the private sector; in most of their remaining activities they do not hold monopoly positions.

In other countries where marketing boards were a problem, reforms were more piecemeal. In many of these countries, steps were taken to improve the financial positions of marketing boards (shedding labor and reducing input subsidies provided through the marketing boards) and to reduce the rigidity with which producer prices are set. The latter often involved moving producer prices closer to world prices or shifting to minimum indicative prices. In a few countries, private participation was introduced in some activities previously monopolized by marketing boards for both exports and domestically consumed goods; limited divestiture took place in two countries. Nevertheless, in all these countries, marketing boards retain a significant degree of monopoly power and producer prices are still administratively controlled or heavily influenced by the marketing board.

Price Controls

In some countries where controls on the availability of goods and foreign exchange were initially widespread, prices were de facto free of control owing to the prevalence of parallel markets. In these countries, removing official controls served mainly to draw parallel market transactions into the official net. Although this process usually enhanced fiscal revenues, its incentive effects on output were comparatively weak. However, when price controls had been less distortive or commodities subject to control had been monopolized by the state, price liberalization had significant real effects on production and consumption decisions.

Substantial progress was made in decontrolling prices, particularly in the agricultural sector, and this change appears to have had positive effects on output. In Bolivia (except for petroleum), Guinea, Madagascar, and Lesotho, prices were largely free prior to the SAF/ESAF programs and remained so throughout the arrangements. In The Gambia, all price controls were lifted during the arrangement. In four other countries (Guyana, Malawi, Niger, and Uganda), price controls on all except a handful of goods considered strategic—principally petroleum and/or utilities—were terminated. For petroleum products, changes in international prices and in the exchange rate were mostly passed on to domestic consumers in a short time. In the remainder of the countries, general controls on prices of goods and on profit margins were abolished and replaced by selective controls.

Exchange and Trade System

Exchange and trade reform—replacing government control over the allocation of foreign exchange with market mechanisms—was the area where most countries were able to make the most forceful changes. In general, the administrative capacity needed to make these changes was less than for many other types of reform. Also, as with price decontrol, reforms to the exchange and trade system tended to meet with relatively little resistance, particularly when a sizable share of the transactions had taken place in parallel markets. In these circumstances, the principal effect of liberalization was to attract foreign exchange flows from parallel markets to official channels, thereby raising government revenues and official foreign exchange receipts. When activity had been more constrained by official controls, the salutary effects of liberalization—particularly strengthening incentives for export production and rationalizing import consumption—were usually quickly evident.

Because exchange and trade restrictions had usually been aimed at officially controlling the allocation of foreign exchange, reforms to exchange and trade systems needed to be supported by changes in exchange rate policy. In the short run, exchange and trade liberalization usually reduced the equilibrium value of domestic currency; however, once the benefits of liberalization had had their full effect on the volume of exports, the equilibrium real exchange rate should have risen. In fact, the countries that undertook the most forceful reforms did devalue or allow the value of their currencies to float down. There has, however, been little sign of any rebound in the equilibrium real exchange rate—probably because of concurrent pressures on the external position from other sources.

Except in the three countries where exchange and trade regimes were broadly free to start with (Bolivia, The Gambia, and Lesotho),[8] exchange and trade reform figured prominently. Bangladesh, Ghana, Guinea, Guyana, and Malawi moved to or close to complete freedom of controls over current international transactions. In Ghana and Guyana, this involved the effective dismantling of the import licensing system while allocating an increasing share of official foreign exchange receipts through market mechanisms—in Ghana, a Dutch auction later supplemented by foreign exchange bureaus, and in Guyana, a legalized parallel market. In these countries, complete unification of exchange markets with full retention of export proceeds was attained during the ESAF period. In Bangladesh, the official and secondary markets were unified through the gradual shifting of transactions from the former to the latter. Malawi and Guinea required less sweeping changes. In Malawi, control over imports through the exchange system was abandoned except for a short negative list of restricted imports, and tariff reform was implemented. And in Guinea, where the trade restrictions had been liberalized during a previous IMF stand-by arrangement, participation in foreign exchange auctions was broadened.

In Mozambique, Tanzania, and Uganda, there had been several earlier but unsuccessful attempts to unify official and parallel market exchange rates through devaluations of the official rate. The SAF and ESAF arrangements aimed at unification through more fundamental systemic changes—principally, introducing or increasing the scope of partial retention of export proceeds and establishing secondary markets for foreign exchange, financed by receipts from nontraditional exports and private transfers. Exchange system reform went the furthest in Uganda, where the parallel market was absorbed into a bureau system, and the few remaining restrictions were generous. However, the exchange rate established in auctions of receipts from donors remained below the bureau exchange rates throughout the arrangement. In Tanzania and Mozambique, there remained considerable, though much reduced, parallel market premia as well as surrender requirements and other controls. In each of these countries, reform of the exchange system was more forceful than that of the trade system. Each introduced or extended the coverage of an open general license system, but this measure generally followed exchange reform and left considerable restrictions and high tariffs in place.

[8]See Appendix Table A4 for a description of these countries. The three others identified in that table as having no major restrictions—Niger, Senegal, and Togo—were members of the WAMU. They retained free exchange systems but restricted trade.

Several countries—Niger, Senegal, Sri Lanka, and Togo—that entered the SAF/ESAF period relatively free of exchange restrictions needed to address still-extensive trade restrictions and to reduce high tariffs. Some progress was made in these areas through the elimination of several quantitative restrictions and reduction and rationalization of tariffs.

Even those countries whose exchange and trade systems were broadly free introduced measures to improve their efficiency. In The Gambia, foreign exchange bureaus were established, and in Bolivia, tariffs were reduced and rationalized. Reform in Lesotho was constrained by its membership in the South African Customs Union.

In several of the ESAF countries, progress made earlier in the reform of the exchange and/or trade system was later set back as delays in receipts from donors tightened the foreign exchange constraint. This back-tracking occurred in Kenya, Madagascar, and Malawi, where previous exchange liberalization was partially reversed or made subject to administrative interference. In two other countries—Burundi and Mauritania—reforms were more piecemeal from the beginning and focused rather narrowly on removing quantitative restrictions on imports or tariff reform while moving to more flexibility in the exchange rate.

In many countries, SAF/ESAF programs also laid the groundwork for promoting foreign direct investment through two principal types of change: first, the propagation of a more stable and liberal macroeconomic environment with avenues for the legal and timely repatriation of profits, and second, changes in the regulatory framework to reduce discrimination against foreign direct investment. There is evidence of some increase in foreign investment in several countries. In many this was directed, in the first instance, to the services sector, especially tourism. Limited investment also took place in agriculture, especially horticulture. Except in Guyana and Bolivia, there is little evidence of increased investment in other tradables. However, real wages in many ESAF countries are low by international standards, and sustained and credible reforms, particularly of the exchange and trade system, should have the potential to attract greater foreign investment.

Exchange Rate Policy

Many of the countries under review had significantly depreciated the nominal value of their currencies during the two years before the SAF/ESAF period, and they had succeeded in depreciating in real terms also but by less than in nominal terms. Nevertheless, there was a perception that in most countries further depreciation was needed, for several reasons: to support ongoing trade and exchange reform; to correct residual overvaluation when previous efforts had been thwarted by inadequately supportive fiscal policies; and to respond to a deterioration in the terms of trade.

Currencies of all countries except those using the CFA franc (Niger, Senegal, and Togo) depreciated during their SAF/ESAF arrangements in nominal terms against the major currencies (Appendix Table A10). However, because several of these currencies—those of Bolivia, Malawi, and Mauritania—depreciated less than other (mainly local) trading partners, they appreciated in nominal effective terms (Table 1 and Appendix Table A11). Movements in the exchange rate of the French franc vis-à-vis currencies of other trading partners caused Togo and Senegal to appreciate in nominal terms and Niger to remain stable. The nominal effective rate for Lesotho remained stable because it is pegged to the South African rand, which dominates in the effective exchange rate weights.

Developments in nominal effective exchange rates were only partially reflected in real effective exchange rates. Although all of the 12 countries that depreciated in nominal effective terms experienced

Table 1. Developments in Effective Exchange Rates
(Annual average percentage change)

Country	SAF Period	ESAF Period	Combined SAF/ESAF Period	Country	SAF Period	ESAF Period	Combined SAF/ESAF Period
I. Countries where nominal effective exchange rates depreciated during their SAF/ESAF arrangements							
Bangladesh				Kenya			
Nominal	−5.4	0.4	−3.5	Nominal	−4.4	−5.2	−5.0
Real	−3.4	−3.8	−3.5	Real	−5.0	−4.0	−4.2
Burundi				Madagascar			
Nominal	−12.1	−2.2	−10.5	Nominal	−29.1	1.2	−12.2
Real	−10.6	0.4	−8.9	Real	−23.0	−4.2	−12.2
Gambia, The				Mozambique			
Nominal	−32.8	3.9	−10.1	Nominal	−62.1	−28.1	−51.0
Real	−12.9	−2.0	−5.8	Real	−36.3	−8.9	−26.5
Ghana				Sri Lanka			
Nominal	−40.4	−10.2	−17.2	Nominal	−10.2	−1.1	−8.0
Real	−22.9	−1.9	−6.5	Real	−1.9	5.3	−0.2
Guinea				Tanzania			
Nominal	−41.7	−28.8	−58.5	Nominal	−28.7	6.9	−22.7
Real	12.2	−19.9	−9.3	Real	−35.6	−1.1	−29.9
Guyana[1]				Uganda			
Nominal	...	−50.6	−50.6	Nominal	−56.6	−36.8	−45.6
Real	...	−21.9	−21.9	Real	7.6	−26.6	−14.5
II. Countries where nominal effective exchange rates appreciated during their SAF/ESAF arrangements							
Bolivia				Senegal			
Nominal	13.4	73.1	59.0	Nominal	5.3	4.4	4.7
Real	−3.6	−5.6	−5.2	Real	1.5	−4.6	−2.6
Malawi[1]				Togo			
Nominal	...	3.4	3.4	Nominal	3.0	8.7	7.2
Real	...	4.5	4.5	Real	−5.8	−2.9	−3.6
Mauritania							
Nominal	1.1	12.9	8.0				
Real	−6.5	−1.2	−3.4				
III. Countries where nominal effective exchange rates were unchanged during their SAF/ESAF arrangements							
Lesotho				Niger			
Nominal	−0.4	−0.1	−0.3	Nominal	−0.9	0.4	−0.1
Real	−1.1	2.0	−0.4	Real	−7.5	−7.1	−7.3

Source: IMF staff estimates.
[1]No SAF arrangement.

Table 2. Money, Interest, and Credit

	Increase in Broad Money (Annual averages, in percent of beginning of period broad money)			Increase in Domestic Credit (Annual averages, in percent of beginning of period broad money)			Interest Rates and Inflation Pre-SAF or Pre-ESAF[4] (In percent)					Interest Rates and Inflation at end-1991 (In percent)				
							Nominal[5]		Real[6]			Nominal[5]		Real[6]		
	Pre-SAF or pre-ESAF[1]	SAF[2]	ESAF[3]	Pre-SAF or pre-ESAF[1]	SAF[2]	ESAF[3]	Loan rate	Deposit rate	Loan rate	Deposit rate	Inflation (CPI)	Loan rate	Deposit rate	Loan rate	Deposit rate	Inflation (CPI)
Bangladesh	28	16	13	30	13	8	16	12	5	—	11	12	11	5	4	7
Bolivia	...	48	45	...	68	63	88	39	13	−16	66	38	19	21	4	15
Burundi	16	7	3	15	6	3	10	7	6	3	4	15	10	6	1	9
Gambia, The	20	32	12	32	−49	−3	20	19	−22	−22	52	26	14	13	2	12
Ghana	62	53	26	63	6	−2	22	21	−9	−10	33	27	20	15	9	10
Guinea[7]	30	30	44	39	15	12	13	15	−31	−30	65	23	20	9	7	12
Guyana	79	...	35	63	...	11	15	13	−44	−45	105	31	29	−28	−29	82
Kenya	17	8	19	23	9	21	14	10	4	—	10	29	15	17	4	10
Lesotho	17	20	1	20	8	−5	14	8	1	−4	13	25	13	9	−1	14
Madagascar	18	19	19	8	−3	−2	13	15	−2	1	15	12	11	3	2	9
Malawi	20	...	14	19	...	—	20	16	4	1	15	18	14	5	1	12
Mauritania	14	10	12	11	11	42	12	9	4	1	8	12	7	8	3	4
Mozambique	15	51	34	26	43	26	20	16	−54	−56	163	34	34	−1	−1	35
Niger	5	9	6	2	−8	−30	10	6	15	11	−4	16	7	15	6	1
Senegal	3	9	3	9	10	−9	11	6	6	1	5	16	7	16	7	—
Sri Lanka	11	16	22	16	21	13	18	10	7	—	10	20	14	10	5	9
Tanzania[7]	20	36	41	35	44	2	19	14	−11	−15	33	26	23	4	1	21
Togo	8	−8	4	7	−2	1	14	5	14	5	—	16	7	15	6	1
Uganda	177	165	56	164	116	49	40	30	−58	−61	237	39	35	9	6	28
Mean (excl. Bolivia and Uganda)	23	21	18	25	8	5	14	12	−6	−9	32	21	15	7	2	15
Median	18	19	19	22	10	3	15	13	4	—	15	23	14	9	4	10

Source: IMF staff estimates.
[1] Average during three years preceding first SAF- or ESAF-supported program.
[2] Average during period from first SAF-supported program to year preceding first ESAF-supported program.
[3] Average during period commencing with first ESAF-supported program.
[4] Interest rates at end of calendar or fiscal year preceding the first SAF- or ESAF-supported program.
[5] Commercial bank loan and time deposit rates. The rate used is a representative rate, the midpoint of published rates, or where available, the weighted average of interest rates.
[6] Real interest rates, given by rr = 100((1 + rn/100)/(1 + cpi/100) − 1) where rr is the real interest rate, rn is the nominal interest rate, and cpi is the CPI inflation rate.
[7] Pre-SAF or pre-ESAF averages are for one year only.

a real effective depreciation during the SAF/ESAF period, only 7 saw real depreciations of more than half the nominal depreciation. In these countries—Bangladesh, Burundi, The Gambia, Kenya, Madagascar, Mozambique, and Tanzania—domestic demand was significantly restrained by relatively large fiscal adjustments and/or by declining export prices. Other influences that are likely to have contributed to substantial real depreciations in some countries were a lack of extensive wage indexing and a relatively large amount of unused labor. These circumstances probably helped contain pressures on wages and consumer prices following the nominal depreciations. Among the seven countries whose currencies appreciated or remained stable in nominal effective terms during their SAF/ESAF arrangements, all except Malawi experienced real effective depreciations. This situation reflected the lower level of inflation in these countries compared with that in trading partners.

For most of the 19 ESAF countries, relative consumer price indices are not always the best indicator of the price incentive for exporters. More accurate indicators are hard to construct, but the ratio of export unit values to the consumer price index (a proxy for domestic costs) can be informative. This measure suggests that in all countries except Lesotho, Malawi, Niger, and Togo, the price incentive to exporters improved, notwithstanding often large deteriorations in the terms of trade (Appendix Table A12). For most countries—even several that experienced the largest terms of trade losses—gains in this more specific indicator of export competitiveness were greater than those in relative consumer price indices. Most of the improvement in the price incentive for exporters occurred in the early years of SAF/ESAF arrangements; since 1989 almost every country has seen a leveling off or slight deterioration in this measure. This trend reflects both some diminution in the depreciation of nominal exchange rates and the more pronounced weakening of export prices for some countries since 1989.

Financial Sector Policies

Under SAF and ESAF arrangements, financial sector policies were aimed at constraining credit growth, especially to the public sector, while enhancing the role of market mechanisms in allocating credit, shifting to indirect means of monetary control, eliminating quasi-fiscal activities of the banking system, and strengthening financial institutions. Virtually all SAF- and ESAF-supported programs had an agenda in these areas, but progress in implementing them generally proved slower than expected. In general, delays arose because of weak technical and administrative capacity; the long time required to develop competitive banking structures; and impediments posed by inadequate reforms in other areas, particularly public enterprises, which banks were often forced to support.

Putting aside Bolivia and Uganda, where extremely rapid money growth was reduced sharply, the growth of broad money in the countries under review remained broadly unchanged from the period prior to SAF/ESAF arrangements; in eight countries, growth diminished (relative to the prior rate) and in another eight, growth increased (Table 2). Developments in domestic credit were heavily affected by progress in reducing the financing requirements of the public sector. The growth of domestic credit dropped or was unchanged in all countries, and the accumulation of foreign assets rose. Conclusions on the composition of credit are not possible, owing to the lack of comparability in the classification of private and public sector credit.

Much progress was made in establishing positive real interest rates. Increases in real lending rates were slightly greater than those on real deposit rates in line with the objective in many SAF/ESAF programs of improving the profitability of banks. Real interest rates on time deposits rose in 16 of the 19 countries during the SAF/ESAF period, but were still negative or barely positive in 6 countries at the end of the period. Most of the latter were high-inflation countries, a fact that underscores the difficulty of establishing positive real interest rates in an inflationary environment. Real loan rates rose or were unchanged in all countries and were positive at the end of the period in all but two. In general, except in Bolivia, The Gambia, Ghana, and Sri Lanka, where interest rates were largely free of control, interest rates were, at least initially, raised administratively. Subsequently, most countries rationalized the structure of interest rates substantially, and three countries—Burundi, Kenya, Malawi—progressed to full liberalization. Even in countries that fully decontrolled interest rates, however, uncompetitive banking structures often prevented proper responses to market forces.

The shift to indirect means of monetary control has progressed more slowly than interest rate liberalization. About half the 19 ESAF countries took significant steps, including changes in reserve requirements, measures to make central bank refinancing more market oriented, the introduction of central bank securities, sometimes with regular auctions, and the development of active secondary markets, interbank markets, and money markets. However, because countries have been reluctant to abandon direct monetary controls until these new systems are tested and trusted, these systems have tended to supplement rather than replace traditional means of control. The IMF has provided extensive

Table 3. Social Indicators

		Population		Health and Nutrition		Urbanization	Education	
	GNP per Capita 1990 (*In US$*)	Average annual growth 1980–90 (*In percent*)	Population aged 0–14 yrs 1990 (*Percent of total*)	Population per physician 1984	Daily calorie supply 1989	Population in urban areas 1990 (*Percent of total*)	Primary net enrollment 1989[1]	Female primary education 1989[2]
Bangladesh	210	2.3	42.9	6,390	2,021	16	63	78
Bolivia	630	2.5	42.5	1,530	1,916	51	83	89
Burundi	210	2.8	45.6	21,020	1,932	6	51	80
Gambia, The	260	...	...	...	...	...	...	...
Ghana	390	3.4	46.8	20,390	2,248	33	...	81
Guinea	440	2.5	46.1	...	2,132	26	26	45
Guyana	330	...	...	...	...	...	...	...
Kenya	370	3.8	49.9	10,050	2,163	24	...	94
Lesotho	530	2.7	43.4	18,610	2,299	20	72	122
Madagascar	230	3.0	45.5	9,780	2,158	25	64	95
Malawi	200	3.4	46.7	11,340	2,139	12	50	81
Mauritania	500	2.4	44.6	11,900	2,685	47	...	69
Mozambique	80	2.6	44.1	...	1,680	27	45	78
Niger	310	3.3	47.2	39,670	2,308	20	17	57
Senegal	710	2.9	46.7	...	2,369	38	48	72
Sri Lanka	470	1.4	32.3	5,520	2,277	21	100	93
Tanzania	110	3.1	46.7	24,970	2,206	33	48	98
Togo	410	3.5	48.1	8,700	2,214	26	72	63
Uganda	220	2.5	48.7	...	2,153	10	...	...
Average	348	2.8	45.2	14,605	2,171	26	57	81
Memorandum items:								
Low-income economies	350	2.0	35.2	5,800	2,406	38	...	78
Middle-income economies	2,220	2.0	35.8	2,250	2,860	60	89	90
High-income economies	19,590	0.6	19.9	470	3,409	77	97	95

Source: World Bank, *World Development Report 1992* (New York: Oxford University Press for the World Bank, 1992).
[1]Percent of children of primary school age actually enrolled.
[2]Females per 100 males enrolled in primary school.

technical assistance in this area, but further development of local expertise is needed.

The elimination of quasi-fiscal activities and improvements in banking practices was slow. Over half the countries reviewed removed quasi-fiscal portfolio restrictions on commercial banks. In some of these, however, selective credit controls and moral suasion over banks' lending practices persist. Officials in many countries were concerned about the vulnerability of certain sectors—particularly agriculture—if preferential credit practices were eliminated.

The restructuring and strengthening of financial institutions was another area where progress was slow. In general, countries were relatively quick to identify institutions requiring restructuring or liquidation and to pass new prudential regulations, but implementation of restructuring or rescue operations was often delayed and enforcement of new regulations proved difficult. One of the important sources of delay in both connections was the continuing demand for credit on the part of weak public enterprises.

Social Dimensions of Adjustment

In view of the low per capita incomes and the inadequate availability of social services in the 19 program countries (Table 3), reform initiatives have paid increasing attention to alleviating poverty and mitigating the social costs of adjustment. The World Bank and the IMF have collaborated in this area; the Fund staff has focused on budgetary and macroeconomic implications and the Bank staff on longer term poverty reduction. The Bank has greatly increased emphasis on mitigating the social costs of adjustment and promoting sustainable poverty reduction strategies. IDA adjustment credits have increasingly specified measures to reduce social costs of adjustment and improve longer term social policies. The IMF has also made efforts to improve policy design and integrate social safety nets in Fund-supported programs.[9]

Increasing production and employment is the only way to reduce poverty in low-income countries for the long term. For most of the ESAF countries—particularly those in Africa, where agriculture is the mainstay of the economy—this often means improving conditions and incentives for agricultural production. Gains in this area for many of the countries may well have been the most significant influence of ESAF programs on poverty. These gains frequently owed much to such structural reforms as increases in agricultural producer prices and reforms affecting marketing boards, which contributed to both higher production and the redistribution of income from rentiers to the poorer rural sector; such benefits were important in Bangladesh, Ghana, Guinea, Niger, Tanzania, Togo, and Uganda. Improvements in infrastructure, such as agricultural extension services, marketing, credit extension, and transportation, also supported the supply response. The lowering of inflation is also likely to have benefited the poor, who typically pay a disproportionate share of the inflation tax.

Notwithstanding the generally favorable effects on the poor of improved macroeconomic performance, adjustment often involved short-term social costs to both the poor and other segments of the population. Measures were built into programs to compensate for these. Where adjustment involved retrenchment of employment in the civil service or public enterprises, severance pay and/or retraining programs were provided in Bolivia, The Gambia, Guinea, Mauritania, Senegal, Sri Lanka, and Uganda. Where subsidies on consumer items were lifted or reduced, these were often replaced by better-targeted assistance in the form of food distribution (Bangladesh, Mozambique, Malawi), food stamps (Sri Lanka), or income supplements for the urban poor (Mozambique). In Lesotho and Kenya, the poor were exempted from increased user fees for health and education. Because weak information bases made it difficult to evaluate the social impact of adjustment, several countries began to improve the data base or analytical framework for such measures.[10]

Many countries also introduced measures specifically directed toward alleviating poverty. The ambitiousness of the measures varied among countries and was typically constrained by limited administrative and financial resources. Several approaches were tried: employment programs, often in labor-intensive public works, to provide work and income to the poor; increased spending on social programs, mainly in health and education with a bias toward expenditures that benefited the poor and rural areas; improvements in the economic and social infrastructure; and, in a few countries, transfers to vulnerable groups, usually in the form of food or cash. The most ambitious scheme of this last sort was the Jana Saviya program in Sri Lanka; others were food grain distribution in Bangladesh, basic health and primary education programs in Bolivia, targeted assistance for the poor in Guyana, agricultural and nutritional programs in Malawi, an outreach program in Lesotho, and income supplements for the urban poor in Mozambique.

[9]Research conducted in the context of the third in-house seminar on poverty has been published in IMF Working Papers on Bangladesh, Sri Lanka, Malawi, and Mozambique. See the list of references.

[10]Household surveys were initiated in Guinea, Guyana, and Mauritania; Kenya set up a National Household Welfare Monitoring Program; in Niger an analytical base was provided by efforts under a United Nations Development Program to reduce the social costs of adjustment; and in Ghana a comprehensive report on the social dimensions of adjustment recommended more direct integration of social issues into the budget and public investment program.

IV External and Domestic Performance: Progress Toward External Viability and Sustained Growth

The structural reforms and macroeconomic policies in ESAF-supported programs were intended to promote two fundamental objectives: to make significant progress toward external viability and to create conditions for sustained growth. The first part of this section assesses the ESAF countries' progress toward external viability—an overall external position and structure of the balance of payments consistent with sustainable inflows of normal financing. The second part assesses progress in creating conditions for sustained growth by reviewing developments in savings and investment, external trade, inflation, and ultimately growth itself. These two objectives for ESAF-supported arrangements—external viability and sustainable economic growth—are mutually supportive and must be assessed jointly. To be sustained, external viability requires resistance to pressure for the growth of absorption to exceed the growth of output, but this resistance is possible only if output and living standards grow at socially acceptable rates. At the same time, strong growth in output will not endure if it relies on unsustainable financing inflows.

Progress Toward External Viability

Most of the 19 countries under review entered the SAF/ESAF period with exceptionally weak external positions. Attaining external viability for them meant not just lowering external borrowing requirements but reducing a large external debt overhang. For most of the countries, these objectives were critical to regaining normal relations with creditors and, eventually, achieving access to commercial financing.

In most of the ESAF countries, conventional criteria for assessing progress toward external viability (Box 2) were not applicable because of the severity of these countries' initial debt problems: none of them had significant access to commercial financing beyond trade credits; nearly all had extremely high (and often rising) debt and debt-service ratios; most had been obliged to reschedule debt; few were meeting all contractual debt-service obligations; and all were resorting to exceptional financing in some form. These characteristics suggest two conclusions. First, traditional indicators of external viability—secondary market prices of debt and access to spontaneous commercial borrowing—were

Box 2. Criteria for Assessing External Viability

There are no clear-cut criteria for assessing external viability because viability depends on the willingness of creditors to finance a country's current account deficits. Often, judgments on viability are based on market tests: access to spontaneous commercial borrowing, developments in secondary market prices of debt, or reliance on exceptional financing. A concept closely related to viability and central to an assessment of medium-term prospects is that of the sustainability of a country's external position—the capacity of a country to finance a continuation of recent trends in the current account deficit without compromising its ability to meet debt-service payments. Sustainability can be evaluated in terms of the evolution of ratios of debt and debt service to some domestic resource base, for example, exports of goods and nonfactor services.[1] When these ratios are rising and/or so high as to render a country unable to meet its contractual debt-service payments, the external position is unlikely to be sustainable; when contractual debt-service obligations are met and debt and debt-service ratios are stable or falling, the external position is more likely to be sustainable.

[1]In this paper debt and debt service are viewed relative to exports rather than GDP for two reasons: first, export data are more accurate and comprehensive than GDP data; and second, changes in real exchange rates, which were large during this period, produce sharp changes in ratios of debt to GDP, reflecting the "capital loss" on debt relative to nontraded goods.

Table 4. Debt-Service Ratios
(In percent of exports of goods and nonfactor services)

	Scheduled Debt-Service Payments				Scheduled Interest Payments			
	Pre-SAF or pre-ESAF[1]	SAF[2]	ESAF[3]	Most recent year[4]	Pre-SAF or pre-ESAF[1]	SAF[2]	ESAF[3]	Most recent year[4]
I. Countries with low or falling debt-service ratios								
Bangladesh	27.4	26.6	20.7	17.6	9.1	8.7	5.8	5.3
Bolivia	84.3	79.6	51.1	49.2	37.0	31.5	22.5	20.0
Gambia, The	27.2	31.0	19.1	15.3	14.3	18.8	8.9	6.3
Ghana	45.6	54.4	45.7	29.5	15.3	13.5	11.7	10.4
Guyana	106.8	...	85.9	59.7	39.7	...	45.3	41.0
Lesotho	4.7	3.8	3.9	3.9	1.5	1.5	1.3	1.3
Malawi	32.7	...	34.7	20.5	17.6	...	12.4	7.1
Mauritania	38.3	38.7	23.2	34.5	13.8	16.0	12.1	11.7
Mozambique[5]	291.3	269.3	197.4	172.8	85.4	91.4	64.3	54.0
Niger	51.2	52.0	50.3	47.3	19.7	20.5	17.6	13.4
Senegal	26.0	33.4	28.7	23.7	12.3	13.6	10.8	9.2
Sri Lanka	26.6	24.8	20.1	20.1	9.3	7.9	7.3	7.3
Tanzania[5]	59.6	49.4	41.5	41.5	21.0	23.0	22.0	22.0
Togo	30.0	21.0	14.8	13.9	11.8	9.1	7.4	6.6
Mean	60.8	57.0	45.7	39.3	22.0	21.3	17.8	15.4
II. Countries with high and rising debt-service ratios								
Burundi	18.7	38.3	30.6	30.6	7.2	13.7	10.1	10.1
Guinea[5]	23.9	27.7	30.4	30.4	8.8	9.7	9.5	9.5
Kenya	30.2	27.5	32.5	33.4	11.3	11.0	11.9	12.6
Madagascar	71.5	83.4	73.9	76.1	38.0	44.3	38.9	38.5
Uganda	44.1	54.4	81.8	102.5	10.5	15.3	29.0	35.8
Mean	37.7	46.3	49.8	54.6	15.2	18.8	19.9	21.3

Source: IMF staff estimates.
[1] Average of three years preceding first SAF- or ESAF-supported program.
[2] Average over period commencing with first SAF-supported program and ending in year before first ESAF-supported program.
[3] Average over period commencing with first ESAF-supported program.
[4] Calendar year 1991 or fiscal 1991/92.
[5] Data available only for one year prior to SAF.

either not applicable or so far out of reach as to be meaningless. Second, in the bulk of the countries, debt burdens—that is, debt stocks relative to the resource base—were excessive, so that making progress toward external viability would certainly entail their reduction.

In these circumstances, two yardsticks for measuring progress toward viability seem appropriate: the extent to which debt-service ratios were reduced, and the reduction in reliance on exceptional financing, defined as the accumulation of arrears to external creditors, rescheduling of interest and/or principal repayments, and balance of payments support from multilateral organizations. Obviously, the two yardsticks are related to one another, since a large or growing debt burden may be an important cause of a country's need for exceptional finance. Conversely, a high or rising debt ratio may be a leading indicator of future recourse to exceptional financing. It is informative, however, to use both yardsticks because a growing recourse to exceptional financing may signal difficulty in obtaining financing in spite of a low or falling debt ratio.

The high level of grants and the concessionality of the ESAF countries' debt raises a further question: even if normal relations with creditors could be established and the debt burden reduced to a sustainable level (given concessional terms), would donors continue to provide grants and concessional financing on the scale experienced in the past? For the countries under review, external viability would be out of reach if financing needs had to be met exclu-

Table 5. Scheduled Debt Service Relative to External Debt
(In percent)

	Effective Nominal Interest Rate[1]				Effective Real Interest Rate[2]				Principal Payments[3]			
	Pre-SAF or pre-ESAF[4]	SAF[5]	ESAF[6]	Most recent year[7]	Pre-SAF or pre-ESAF[4]	SAF[5]	ESAF[6]	Most recent year[7]	Pre-SAF or pre-ESAF[4]	SAF[5]	ESAF[6]	Most recent year[7]
I. Denominated in SDRs												
Gambia, The	4.2	5.4	3.8	3.3	21.5	2.5	0.9	2.5	3.9	3.5	4.5	4.7
Kenya	5.7	4.9	5.3	5.5	14.3	−0.4	8.0	6.2	9.4	7.3	9.2	9.1
Lesotho	2.5	2.6	2.0	2.0	−1.3	2.8	0.1	0.1	5.3	4.2	4.1	4.1
Madagascar	6.5	6.1	6.0	5.4	9.9	25.0	14.1	13.4	4.5	...	6.5	4.7
Malawi	5.1	...	3.6	2.5	9.2	...	−1.8	−5.3	5.8	5.4	5.4	5.3
Mauritania	3.9	4.5	4.0	3.7	3.1	8.5	1.0	−3.3	7.0	6.3	3.4	7.1
Mean	4.6	4.7	4.1	3.8	9.4	6.4	3.7	2.3	6.0	5.3	5.5	5.8
Market rate (SDR)[8]	8.5	7.5	7.8	7.7								
II. Denominated in U.S. dollars												
Bangladesh	2.2	2.0	1.4	1.3	5.3	−2.2	−0.1	1.2	4.3	4.1	3.6	3.1
Bolivia	7.6	5.1	4.6	4.7	15.0	12.3	7.5	13.6	9.7	7.8	6.0	6.8
Burundi	2.3	2.2	1.3	1.3	−1.1	9.1	0.9	0.9	3.7	3.9	2.6	2.6
Ghana	4.8	4.2	3.6	3.3	4.6	1.8	9.7	6.3	9.7	12.8	10.6	6.0
Guinea	5.8	3.4	3.4	3.4	5.8	0.2	11.7	11.7	4.9	6.3	7.4	7.4
Guyana	2.9	...	5.2	5.2	4.7	...	0.9	5.5	8.3	...	4.6	2.4
Mozambique	4.7	4.6	3.6	3.5	−3.6	4.1	0.8	0.9	11.3	9.0	7.6	7.6
Sri Lanka	4.1	3.6	3.6	3.6	9.6	1.4	2.7	2.7	7.5	7.7	6.3	6.3
Tanzania	3.7	4.3	3.8	3.8	7.4	4.1	9.2	9.2	6.8	4.9	3.3	3.3
Uganda	3.9	4.1	3.3	3.4	4.1	37.8	23.3	14.7	12.8	10.5	5.9	6.3
Mean	4.2	3.7	3.4	3.4	5.2	7.6	6.6	6.6	7.9	7.4	5.8	5.2
Market rate (U.S. dollar)[8]	10.0	8.5	8.0	7.7								
III. Denominated in CFA francs												
Niger	7.2	6.6	4.5	3.4	8.7	9.0	14.1	7.3	11.5	10.2	8.4	8.6
Senegal	5.0	4.7	4.6	4.5	4.0	10.7	−0.5	1.1	5.5	6.8	7.6	7.1
Togo	5.9	5.0	4.6	4.1	13.1	6.6	2.5	0.8	9.1	6.5	4.5	4.5
Mean	6.0	5.4	4.6	4.0	8.6	8.8	5.4	3.1	8.7	7.8	6.8	6.7
Market rate (French franc)[8]	10.6	8.5	8.0	7.7								
Overall mean	4.6	4.3	3.8	3.6	7.1	7.8	5.5	4.7	7.4	6.9	5.9	5.6

Sources: International Monetary Fund, *International Financial Statistics* yearbook (Washington), various issues; and IMF staff estimates.
[1]Interest due in percent of debt stock.
[2]Deflated by export prices.
[3]Principal payments due in percent of debt stock.
[4]Average over three years preceding first SAF- or ESAF-supported program.
[5]Average during period from first SAF-supported program to year preceding first ESAF-supported program.
[6]Average during period from first ESAF-supported program to present.
[7]Calendar year 1991 or fiscal year 1991/92.
[8]Long-term government bond rates as reported in *International Financial Statistics*. The rate for the SDR is proxied by a simple average of long-term bond rates in the United States, France, and Japan. The rates reported are averages across countries of the rates in effect during the relevant periods.

sively by debt on market-related terms. Thus, progress toward viability is assessed here in terms of reducing debt and debt-service burdens to manageable levels, assuming that concessional inflows and grants will remain important.

Evolution of Debt-Service Burdens

Measuring the debt burden in the ESAF countries presents several problems. The conventional index of the debt burden—the stock of debt relative to the resource base—fails to capture the effect of debt relief in the form of more concessional terms: lower interest rates and longer grace and repayment periods. For this reason, an attractive alternative for ESAF countries would be to compare the present value of future debt-service commitments with the present value of future export receipts. This approach, however, suffers from its sensitivity to the discount rate assumed (which should be greater than the concessional, effective interest rate on debt), the uncertainty about future export receipts, and the exceptionally complex data requirements for the calculation. Moreover, in many of the ESAF countries, the immediate problem is to reduce the cash flow on debt service.[11]

This paper, therefore, views the debt burden in terms of the ratios of scheduled total debt-service payments (i.e., principal plus interest) to exports and the ratio of scheduled interest payments to exports. These measures are readily accessible and capture changes in concessionality. It is useful to look at both ratios because they measure different aspects of the debt burden: the *debt service to exports ratio* reflects the gross impact of debt on foreign exchange cash flow, while the *interest to exports ratio* measures the economic cost of the debt. (When principal payments are routinely rolled over, the interest ratio is also a good measure of the net impact of debt on the foreign exchange cash flow.) In the present context, the two measures generally tell the same story, both because they were influenced in the same way by developments in exports and because increases in the concessionality of interest rates were typically reinforced by lengthened repayment periods.

Most of the ESAF countries showed significant progress in reducing their debt-service burdens (Table 4). In 14 countries the debt-service ratio either fell below its level prior to the SAF/ESAF period or—for Lesotho—remained very low after a slight increase; in 8, the ratio fell by more than a third. In five countries, however, the debt-service ratio increased, in a few by large amounts. The changes in the ratios of interest to exports were less pronounced—but in the same direction—as those in the debt-service ratio except in Guyana and Tanzania, where there were large reductions in the debt-service ratio but not in the interest ratio.[12]

Why did some countries succeed in reducing their debt-service ratios while others did not? To what extent did these outcomes reflect changes in lending terms of creditors, increases in export prices, or the fruits of adjustment policies? These questions are best approached by splitting changes in the debt-service ratio into two components: changes in the ratio of debt service to debt (which corresponds rather closely to changes in the terms on debt) and changes in the ratio of debt to exports. The rest of this section examines the evolution of these components for the countries under review. Its broad conclusion is that while all benefited from more favorable lending terms, the principal differences among them were in the evolution of export prices and the results of adjustment policies.

Terms of Borrowing

All 19 ESAF countries received concessional interest rates: effective interest rates (measured as the ratio of scheduled interest payments to debt) were typically about 4 percentage points below long-term market rates during the ESAF period (Table 5). Moreover, during the SAF/ESAF period as a whole, effective interest rates fell for all the countries except Guyana. For most countries, this drop was less than the parallel decline in long-term market interest rates in creditor countries, although for a few it was considerably larger. Much of the variation among the ESAF countries in the spread between effective and market interest rates reflected their different choices from the menu of Paris Club options available under the so-called Trinidad terms and enhanced concessions. Ex post real effective interest rates—measured in terms of changes in export unit values—also fell on average, although again there was a wide range of developments; in general, this drop reflected both the drop in the nominal interest rate and the fact that export prices had fallen prior to the SAF/ESAF period by even more than they did during the period.

Longer grace periods and maturities of new borrowing and rescheduling brought about a reduction in the ratio of principal payments to debt in all but

[11]A variant of this measure—the ratio of the present value of future debt-service payments to current exports—is presented in World Bank, *Adjustment in Africa: Progress, Payoffs and Challenges,* World Bank Policy Research Report No. 2 (forthcoming).

[12]In Guyana, the pronounced drop in principal payments mainly reflects a change in the treatment of commercial bank debt past due. In Tanzania, the decline in principal was the lagged effect of reduced borrowing in the early 1980s.

four countries.[13] The average reduction amounted to about 2 percentage points and, therefore, quantitatively contributed more than lower interest rates to the reduction in debt-service ratios. While this drop simply reflected a shift toward greater back-loading of repayment schedules, the fact that all countries were borrowing at below-market interest rates meant that any lengthening in repayment periods increased the grant component of borrowing.

Evolution of Debt Ratios

The evolution of the ratio of debt to exports (even calculated at the face value rather than present value) is critical to the countries under review for two reasons: first, given the limited scope for more concessional terms, restoring debt-service ratios to manageable levels almost always requires a reduction in the debt ratio; and second, once debt-service ratios reach a manageable level, sustainability requires a stable ratio of debt to exports, assuming unchanged terms on new debt.

During the SAF/ESAF period, ratios of debt to exports fell in almost half of the countries under review. Specifically, in 8 of the 19, debt ratios fell, reversing what had been (except in Togo) an increasing trend (Chart 8). These eight countries were fairly evenly spread across the spectrum of debt distress prior to the SAF/ESAF period: Bangladesh, The Gambia, Malawi, Senegal, and Togo were among the better-positioned countries in terms of the level of debt and their records on debt servicing at the outset of the period, but Bolivia, Guyana, and Mozambique were among the most heavily indebted. In another five countries, debt ratios were stabilized after years of increases. In the six remaining countries, debt ratios continued to rise. However, in a few, debt and debt-service ratios had been quite low at the outset of the SAF/ESAF period owing to creditors' reluctance to lend when economic policies were weak. The strengthening of policies during arrangements with the IMF prompted a resumption of lending that pushed up debt and debt-service ratios.

The conventional framework for evaluating the sustainability of debt (Box 3) indicates four sources of changes in the ratio of debt to exports: (1) the cancellation of debt maturing in the future, (2) the growth of exports of goods and services relative to the effective interest rate on external debt, (3) the accumulation of new debt owing to an excess of the primary current account deficit and accumulation of reserves over non-debt-creating inflows, and (4) changes in the exchange rates between a numeraire currency and the currencies in which debt is actually denominated. These influences and the resulting change in debt ratios are shown in Table 6 and Appendix Table A13.[14] From these tables, four broad conclusions emerge.

Chart 8. Gross External Debt
(End of period; percent of exports)

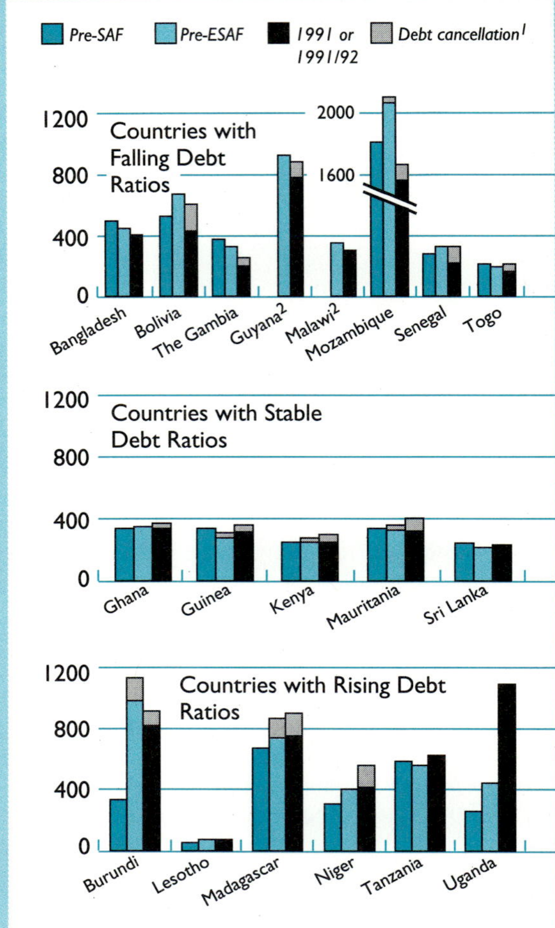

[1]Ratio of debt to exports that would have resulted if there had been no debt cancellation.
[2]No SAF arrangement.

[13]The ratio of principal due to total debt is a very rough indicator of repayment terms. Its inverse would be a robust index of the average maturity of a country's debt if the maturity structure of the debt were unchanging. Since this is not the case, this measure is merely suggestive of changes in maturity.

[14]An important caveat in interpreting these data is that the correspondence between changes in recorded debt and changes implied by balance of payments flows is often poor.

Box 3. Evolution of the Ratio of Debt to Exports

The influences underlying movements in the ratio of debt to exports can be viewed in a framework familiar from assessing the sustainability of domestic public debt. This framework derives from a basic identity expressing the change in the value of gross debt (B) in terms of six components: the noninterest current account deficit ($NICAD$); official grants and other net non-debt-creating inflows (NDC); debt cancellation (F); the accumulation of gross official reserves (ΔR); nominal interest payments (iB_{t-1}); and a cross exchange rate term ΔCE to capture the effects of changes in the exchange rates between the numeraire currency and other currencies in which a country's debt is denominated.

$$(1)\quad B_t - B_{t-1} = NICAD_t - NDC_t - F_t + \Delta R_t + i_t B_{t-1} + \Delta CE_t$$

Expressing debt as a percent of export values and taking percentage changes produces an expression that permits the easy classification of the factors contributing to the rate of increase in the debt ratio ($\hat{b}_t$).

$$(2)\quad \hat{b}_t = \frac{NICAD_t - NDC_t - F_t + \Delta R_t}{B_{t-1}} + (i_t - g_t) + \frac{\Delta CE_t}{B_{t-1}} - Z_t$$

where g is the increase in export values and Z is a sum of cross-product terms. In Table 6 the increase in export values is separated into price and volume components.

First, in most of the eight countries that managed to reduce their debt ratios, more than 10 percent of the initial stock of debt was canceled; in four of these countries, debt cancellation was sufficient, or more than sufficient, to account for the total reduction in the debt ratios.[15] Notably, however, significant debt cancellation, equivalent to over 10 percent of initial debt, also took place in the countries where the debt ratio increased or was roughly unchanged. Thus, while debt cancellation was a central determinant of the reductions in debt ratios that occurred, it did not differ significantly between countries that reduced their debt burdens and those that did not.

Second, what did differ significantly between the two groups of countries was the growth of exports of goods and services—the change in the resource base against which debt is measured in this analysis. Both volume and price developments contributed to the large differences in export growth across countries. In countries where debt ratios fell, export volume growth averaged almost 7 percent annually—more than three times the rate in the countries where debt ratios rose. The divergence in export price changes was even larger. Export prices rose at an annual rate in excess of 2 percent in the countries where debt ratios fell, compared with an annual decline of 5½ percent in countries where ratios rose. In fact, among the six countries where export prices fell over the period, only Bolivia and Ghana managed to avoid an increase in their debt ratios.

Third, noninterest current account positions—excluding grants—were on average stronger in countries where debt ratios fell or remained stable than in countries where they rose. Since exports were the principal factor differentiating the evolution of current account positions, this was a second channel through which export growth affected debt ratios. Although grants and other non-debt-creating inflows provided some offset—such inflows tended to be highest in countries with the largest deficits before grants—the offset was less than complete. Thus, differences between the three groups of countries in noninterest current accounts including grants were also significant.

Fourth, effective interest rates on external debt and changes in debt valuation owing to variations in cross exchange rates were broadly similar across the groupings of countries.

Sustainability of Debt

The assessment of debt ratios thus far has focused on how the evolution of these ratios affected the debt-service ratio and what were the sources of changes in the debt ratio. Another important question is whether the countries under review were able to create conditions in which the ratio of debt to exports would be stable without any further cancellation of debt. Even if a country was able to attain a manageable debt-service ratio, this progress would lack a sound foundation if new borrowing

[15] Table 6 shows average annual changes in variables—identified in Box 3—that affected the debt ratio. Appendix Table A13 provides a different presentation, highlighting the cumulative influences of each variable on the debt ratio. Thus, including the residual discrepancy, which captures cross-product terms, the sum of the effects on the debt ratio listed in that table equals the change in the debt ratio.

Table 6. Analysis of Change in External Debt to Export Ratios

	External Debt to Exports[1]			Influences on External Debt to Export Ratio During SAF/ESAF Period (*Annual averages, in percent*)								
	Prior to first SAF or ESAF[2]	Most recent year[2]	Percent change[3]	Non-interest current account deficit[4]	Official grants and other non-debt-creating flows[4,5]	Debt cancel-lation[4,5]	Increase in gross reserves[4]	Effective interest rate[6]	Cross exchange rate changes[7]	Export volume growth[3]	Export price increase[3]	Number of years
I. Countries with falling debt ratios[8]												
*Gambia, The	381	207	−9.7	10.8	−18.7	−1.4	5.0	3.9	−1.4	6.8	2.8	6
*Guyana	903	775	−7.4	1.8	−2.9	−6.6	1.6	5.2	1.7	3.5	4.3	2
*Togo	212	166	−5.9	10.5	−12.0	−3.3	2.0	4.2	−1.8	4.0	1.4	4
*Bolivia	523	422	−4.2	6.9	−6.3	−8.9	—	4.7	1.6	7.8	−2.2	5
*Senegal	271	215	−3.8	9.1	−6.0	−4.2	1.3	4.1	−2.8	1.0	0.7	6
*Malawi	345	297	−3.7	20.3	−17.5	−0.8	0.4	4.0	−0.3	7.2	5.4	4
*Bangladesh	493	406	−3.2	13.5	−7.4	—	2.7	2.3	3.5	9.7	2.9	6
*Mozambique	1,816	1,566	−2.9	20.6	−14.9	−3.6	1.5	5.2	—	12.2	3.1	5
Mean	618	507	−5.1	11.7	−10.7	−3.6	1.8	4.2	0.1	6.6	2.3	5
II. Countries with stable debt ratios[8]												
*Sri Lanka	225	216	−1.0	9.9	−7.5	—	2.5	4.7	0.6	5.6	2.1	4
Kenya	239	231	−0.9	9.5	−7.8	−3.8	−0.5	5.2	−0.3	1.8	1.6	4
Guinea	305	293	−0.8	11.2	−5.7	−2.7	1.1	3.6	—	4.3	1.1	5
*Mauritania	328	323	−0.3	8.0	−7.1	−3.5	0.1	3.6	−1.2	−2.0	0.5	5
*Ghana	331	338	0.4	8.7	−8.5	−2.9	3.2	4.0	1.8	9.8	−3.1	5
Mean	286	280	−0.5	9.4	−7.3	−2.6	1.3	4.2	0.2	3.9	0.4	5
III. Countries with rising debt ratios[8]												
*Tanzania	568	611	1.5	14.3	−13.0	−0.1	1.7	3.5	3.8	0.4	2.0	5
Madagascar	664	732	2.0	3.0	−3.6	−3.4	−0.2	5.5	−0.9	6.4	−6.8	5
*Lesotho	52	65	5.8	125.2	−120.6	−0.3	11.8	3.0	0.6	4.5	0.3	4
*Niger	295	395	6.0	13.3	−10.6	−6.7	0.2	5.1	−1.8	0.1	−6.0	5
Burundi	352	819	15.1	38.6	−27.2	−4.6	4.5	3.2	3.3	2.4	−3.6	6
Uganda	273	1,092	32.0	23.1	−12.4	−0.3	0.5	4.9	2.4	1.2	−13.9	5
Mean (excluding Lesotho)	430	730	11.3	18.5	−13.4	−3.0	1.4	4.4	1.4	2.1	−5.6	5
Overall mean	451	482	1.0	18.9	−16.3	−3.0	2.1	4.2	0.5	4.6	−0.4	5

Source: IMF staff estimates.
Note: Countries marked with an asterisk (*) have a low or falling debt-service ratio.
[1]Stock of medium- and long-term external public and publicly guaranteed debt (including use of IMF resources) as percent of exports of goods and nonfactor services.
[2]End of calendar or fiscal year. Most recent year is 1991 or 1991/92.
[3]Annual average using geometric mean.
[4]Average flow during SAF/ESAF period as percent of debt stock prior to first SAF- or ESAF-supported program. Negative numbers denote net inflows.
[5]Debt reduction affecting current maturities is included in official grants and other non-debt-creating inflows.
[6]Average interest due during period as percent of initial debt stock.
[7]Average changes in cross exchange rates over SAF/ESAF period as percent of initial debt stock. Negative numbers denote depreciations of currency values relative to the numeraire.
[8]Countries listed in ascending order of the annual percent change in their debt to export ratios.

increased the debt stock faster than exports were growing. The framework presented in Box 3 suggests that, for the debt ratio to remain stable in the absence of debt cancellation, of changes in cross exchange rates, or of the need to raise foreign exchange reserve ratios, the excess of the noninterest current account deficit over non-debt-creating inflows must be offset by the excess of export growth over the effective interest rate.

Table 6 indicates that this criterion for the sustainability of the external position was met by ten countries—including all countries except Senegal that experienced declines in their actual debt ratios, as well as Ghana, Lesotho, and Sri Lanka. In each of these countries, the growth in the value of exports exceeded the nominal interest rate; in some, non-debt-creating inflows also exceeded the noninterest current account. These facts should not lead to the conclusion that debt positions were sustainable—several of these countries still had unmanageable debt-service burdens. However, the countries did achieve external current account positions and export growth rates that, given the levels of non-debt-creating inflows and concessional interest rates, would have stabilized or reduced the debt ratio even without debt cancellation. This achievement is important because if such a relationship between these variables could be sustained, any progress in reducing the debt-service ratio—for example, through the cancellation of debt—would not be eroded by a renewed accumulation of debt.

Reliance on Exceptional Financing

How have the changes in debt and debt-service ratios affected countries' abilities to restore or maintain orderly relations with creditors and to finance current account deficits with normal capital inflows? Although the use of ESAF resources is itself a resort to exceptional finance, the need for other forms of exceptional finance should diminish as countries' debt burdens become more manageable. Table 7 shows, for the SAF/ESAF period, developments in countries' reliance on the main forms of exceptional financing: the net accumulation of arrears, rescheduling, the gross use of IMF resources, and gross adjustment lending by the World Bank. At the broadest level, overall reliance on exceptional financing measures the extent to which a country's financing needs exceed normal inflows. More narrowly, the gap between actual and contractual debt-service payments, which is equal to the sum of rescheduling and the net accumulation of arrears, measures the extent to which countries were unable to make debt-service payments on schedule. Finally, the accumulation of arrears represents the most disorderly form of exceptional financing and is a signal of acute difficulties. Broadly, these data provide yardsticks against which to determine whether reductions in debt and debt-service ratios have been sufficient to enable countries to return to normal relations with creditors.

As might be expected, countries that succeeded in lowering debt-service ratios during the SAF/ESAF period also tended to reduce their reliance on exceptional financing. Among the 14 countries with low or falling debt-service ratios, the reliance on exceptional financing fell in 8 countries and was held at a relatively low level in 4 others; the gap between contractual and actual debt-service payments increased significantly in only 2 countries, both of which accumulated arrears. Conversely, the reliance on exceptional financing rose or remained high in all 5 countries with a high or rising debt-service ratio; most of these countries also experienced an increase in the gap between contractual and actual debt-service payments.

Overall Progress Toward Viability: Where Do We Stand?

A joint assessment of debt-service ratios and the reliance on exceptional financing suggests that 11 of the 19 countries under review made visible progress toward external viability.[16] The success in these countries was attributable to both increased concessions on debt (cancellation and easier terms) and, in most countries, strong export growth. For the remaining eight countries, a combination of high or rising ratios of debt, interest payments, and debt service to exports and high or rising reliance on exceptional finance indicate little or no progress in relieving external pressures. Prospects for these countries are mixed. Most of these countries were among those that suffered serious deteriorations in their terms of trade and/or had difficulties sustaining reform efforts.

Developments in Official Grants

Grants represent one end of the spectrum of concessional inflows, and their evolution is complementary to any consideration of debt and debt-service burdens. For the countries under review, increased concessions on debt during the SAF/ESAF period were accompanied by an increase in

[16]Bangladesh, Bolivia, The Gambia, Ghana, Guyana, Lesotho, Malawi, Mozambique, Senegal, Sri Lanka, and Togo. These are the countries that (a) reduced their debt-service ratios (or maintained them at very low levels), (b) reduced (or maintained at low levels) their resort to exceptional financing, and (c) had no significant accumulation of arrears during the ESAF period.

Table 7. Exceptional Financing

(In percent of exports of goods and nonfactor services)

	Exceptional Financing[1]			Contractual Minus Actual Debt-Service Payments[2]			Change in Arrears			
	Pre-SAF or pre-ESAF[3]	SAF[4]	ESAF[5]	Pre-SAF or pre-ESAF[3]	SAF[4]	ESAF[5]	Pre-SAF or pre-ESAF[3]	SAF[4]	ESAF[5]	Stock of arrears[6]
I. Countries with low or falling debt-service ratios										
Bangladesh	6.1	4.8	5.0	—	—	—	—	—	—	—
Bolivia	68.1	43.8	17.2	58.1	44.3	10.5	29.2	−0.9	−12.7	22.7
Gambia, The	19.3	−12.9	−3.2	23.7	−23.4	−7.3	23.7	−26.8	−7.3	—
Ghana	12.7	−3.9	7.4	−13.2	−7.9	−2.5	−13.2	−7.9	−2.5	—
Guyana	96.6	...	48.4	72.2	...	23.3	−1.8	...	−82.6	45.2
Lesotho	—	0.9	1.1	—	—	—	—	—	—	—
Malawi	−12.4	...	12.2	5.9	...	2.2	4.6	...	−2.9	—
Mauritania	21.3	19.2	19.3	14.8	15.6	18.1	−5.2	3.7	11.8	31.0
Mozambique	278.3	257.0	197.2	278.3	230.5	174.4	187.6	−37.2	−92.2	386.2
Niger	25.9	19.7	26.6	17.1	12.7	26.6	—	—	8.5	26.9
Senegal	5.8	9.6	12.7	8.9	7.0	11.2	0.3	−0.5	0.6	2.3
Sri Lanka	−5.2	3.7	6.3	—	—	—	—	—	—	—
Tanzania	40.1	42.3	44.8	35.4	33.1	24.3	−78.7	2.2	−14.0	14.0
Togo	15.8	10.2	10.7	9.4	7.0	8.3	6.1	−17.6	0.9	7.1
Mean	40.9	32.9	29.0	36.5	26.6	20.7	10.9	−7.1	−13.7	38.2
Excluding Mozambique	22.6	12.5	16.0	17.9	8.0	8.8	−2.7	−4.3	−7.7	11.5
II. Countries with high and rising debt-service ratios										
Burundi	—	20.1	12.9	—	—	—	—	—	—	—
Guinea[7]	13.2	11.5	15.3	10.5	9.7	11.0	32.1	3.0	1.2	40.2
Kenya	−5.3	6.9	7.3	—	—	0.4	—	—	0.4	1.2
Madagascar	50.3	49.7	44.5	47.8	47.6	41.4	−2.4	−3.6	7.6	38.3
Uganda	15.1	28.8	60.4	0.5	19.9	25.0	−6.1	8.0	21.7	45.5
Mean	14.7	23.4	28.1	11.8	15.4	15.6	4.7	1.5	6.2	25.0
Overall mean	34.0	30.1	28.7	30.0	23.3	19.3	9.3	−4.6	−8.5	34.8
Excluding Mozambique	20.4	15.9	19.4	16.2	10.4	10.7	−0.6	−2.5	−3.9	15.2

Source: IMF staff estimates.

[1]Net arrears accumulation and use of IMF resources plus gross rescheduling and World Bank adjustment lending. Negative when arrears reduction and repayments to the IMF exceed rescheduling and World Bank adjustment lending.

[2]Net arrears accumulation plus rescheduling. Negative when arrears reduction exceeds rescheduling.

[3]Year preceding first SAF- or ESAF-supported program.

[4]Average over period commencing with first SAF-supported program and ending in year before first ESAF-supported program.

[5]Average over period commencing with first ESAF-supported program.

[6]Calendar year 1991 or fiscal year 1991/1992. Arrears are at end of period.

[7]Guinea's arrears are as of December 1991. Arrears were cleared in November 1992.

the flow of grants: the ratio of grants to imports rose from an average of 23 percent in the year before SAF/ESAF arrangements to 28 percent on average during the ESAF programs (Table 8). However, the increase in aid flows was not uniform: the ratio fell in eight countries, while increases were exceptionally large in several others (Burundi, Mozambique, and Uganda).

Declines in grants relative to imports cannot be interpreted as an unambiguous sign of a less-pronounced need for aid. In several countries, such developments indicate slippages in adjustment programs or project implementation that slowed aid inflows. In countries where grants rose rapidly—Mozambique and Uganda—the reverse process was at play: a strengthening of adjustment and reform encouraged donors to support the rebuilding of urgently needed infrastructure. Indeed, in light of the investment needs in most of the countries under review, external support for development is likely to remain high as long as adjustment and reform efforts provide assurance that funds can be used efficiently.

Table 8. Official Grants
(As a percent of imports)

	Pre-SAF or Pre-ESAF[1]	SAF[2]	ESAF[3]	Most Recent Year[4]
Bangladesh	23.1	23.0	19.4	18.9
Bolivia	12.2	13.5	15.9	16.1
Burundi	52.4	71.0	93.2	93.2
Gambia, The	42.1	43.3	27.0	24.3
Ghana	16.1	13.1	18.6	17.2
Guinea	10.0	15.3	15.9	15.9
Guyana	3.3	...	4.8	3.7
Kenya	7.5	12.3	10.0	10.3
Lesotho	18.1	18.2	18.7	18.7
Madagascar	37.2	34.9	35.0	28.6
Malawi	11.8	...	29.1	18.6
Mauritania	26.8	25.8	24.2	21.1
Mozambique	34.5	48.9	53.5	55.8
Niger	40.7	34.1	39.0	39.4
Senegal	18.0	21.5	21.8	19.3
Sri Lanka	8.7	8.1	6.7	6.7
Tanzania	39.6	39.7	39.4	39.4
Togo	21.9	14.4	17.4	14.9
Uganda	7.8	20.1	38.2	51.2
Mean	22.7	26.9	27.8	27.0

Source: IMF staff estimates.
[1] Year preceding first SAF- or ESAF-supported program.
[2] Average during period from first SAF-supported program to year preceding first ESAF-supported program.
[3] Average during period from first ESAF-supported program to present.
[4] Calendar year 1991 or fiscal year 1991/92.

Domestic Economic Performance

In most of the 19 ESAF countries, the conditions that had given rise to an excessive accumulation of external debt had also produced adverse domestic developments—rising inflation, low savings and investment, and weak efficiency and output growth. Consequently, successful efforts to improve a country's external position were likely to go hand in hand with a strengthening of domestic conditions; this would create a virtuous circle, in which the easing of the external constraint would feed domestic recovery and export growth, which would further ease the external constraint. However, other scenarios were possible, and two were of particular concern. First, if efforts to move toward external viability were to focus disproportionately on demand restraint, improvements in the debt position could come at the cost of domestic growth and investment. In this case, domestic developments would be likely to prove unsustainable, and any progress toward external viability would be short-lived. Second, without adequate financial or structural adjustment, additional external financing (for example, related to an IMF-supported program) would foster an increase in demand and output but fail to strengthen debt-servicing capacity.

Overall Developments

In fact, most indicators of economic performance improved during the SAF/ESAF period (Table 9). Real GDP growth, which averaged about 2 percent a year prior to the respective SAF/ESAF periods, rose to 4 percent during SAF arrangements and 3 percent during the ESAF arrangements.[17] Average export volume growth increased from around 2 percent to around 7 percent. Official reserves rose markedly. And average inflation, while remaining at double-digit levels, fell by one-fifth.

The average current account deficit widened, mainly on account of deteriorating terms of trade but also because of large increases in investment in a few countries. The increase in current account deficits reflected a rise in the average savings rate of a little over 1 percentage point, but an even larger increase in the average investment rate. Developments in investment ratios, however, were highly diverse; exceptionally large increases occurred in

[17] As noted previously, national accounts data in ESAF countries are poor. Therefore, ratios to GDP and cross-country comparisons should be treated with caution.

Table 9. Indicators of Economic Performance
(Annual averages for 19 ESAF countries, in percent, unless otherwise noted)

	Pre-SAF or Pre-ESAF[1]	SAF	ESAF	Most Recent Year[2]
Real GDP growth	2.1	4.0	2.8	2.9
Export volume growth	2.2	4.4	7.3	7.3
Inflation[3]	16.9	15.0	13.3	17.6
Savings/GDP	6.9	8.7	8.5	10.2
Investment/GDP	14.9	18.5	20.7	19.7
Current account/GDP[4]	−12.3	−15.4	−18.0	−16.8
Reserves (months of imports)	2.3	2.9	3.3	3.5
Terms of trade (improvement = +)	0.3	−5.7	−3.9	0.9

[1] Average over three years preceding the first SAF- or ESAF-supported arrangement.
[2] Calendar year 1991 or fiscal year 1991/92.
[3] Excluding Bolivia and Uganda.
[4] Excluding official transfers.

Lesotho, Mozambique, and Uganda, while changes were modest in most others. The largest improvements in each of these indicators occurred in countries that undertook forceful structural reform and that suffered the least from weakening terms of trade.

During the SAF/ESAF period, there was also some progress in addressing the vulnerability of the economies to their highly concentrated export bases (Table 10). On average, a single export accounted for 55 percent, and the leading two commodities for more than 70 percent, of export receipts in the year prior to the first SAF or ESAF program. Two responses to these conditions were needed: first, particularly when the high concentration ratios were due to narrowly focused comparative advantage, reserves needed to be accumulated to cushion the effects of unanticipated fluctuations in the terms of trade or weather; and second, to the extent that concentration stemmed from a distorted incentive structure, reforms were needed to remove disincentives to diversification. Progress in increasing official reserves was significant and broad-based; all but four countries increased the import cover of international reserves, and the average rose from 2.4 to 3.5 months of imports. Likewise, all but four countries increased their reserve cushions relative to the size of a typical fluctuation in foreign exchange receipts, as measured by the standard deviation of exports. Less was accomplished, however, on diversification. Although average export concentration ratios fell, most of the reductions occurred in countries that suffered a drop in export prices. In several countries, there are significant exports of nonfactor services such as tourism, so concentration ratios understate the diversity of foreign exchange receipts. Nevertheless, there is little evidence of an increasing relative role for the services sector.

The preceding paragraphs have reviewed developments through 1991 or 1991/92—the most recent year for which actual data are available. Preliminary data for 1992 paint a mixed picture of more recent performance. This appears to reflect the further deterioration in the terms of trade for many of the 19 countries, the negative effects of drought in sub-Saharan Africa, and in a few countries some slippage in policies.[18] The countries most affected by the drought experienced a contraction of GDP, sharply reduced export volume growth, increasing fiscal and external current account imbalances, and rising inflation. Estimates suggest, however, that the other countries had some increase in GDP growth, roughly unchanged fiscal and external balances, and reduced inflation. In most countries, the ratio of debt to exports rose relative to 1991 levels; the exceptions were four countries where high export volume growth was sustained in the face of worsened terms of trade. While these data are still preliminary they do underscore the vulnerability of these countries to exogenous shocks and policy setbacks. Recent developments in some countries have also been affected by the importance that donors place on good governance in sustaining aid inflows.

[18]This discussion is based on a combination of preliminary data and recent short-term projections for the 13 countries whose data are on a calendar-year basis: Bolivia, Burundi, Ghana, Guinea, Guyana, Kenya, Madagascar, Malawi, Mauritania, Mozambique, Niger, Sri Lanka, and Togo.

Table 10. Resiliency of Export Revenues

	Most Important Export Commodities by Share of Total Exports	Shares of the Two Top Exports: Prior to SAF/ESAF (In percent of exports)			Shares of the Two Top Exports: Most recent year (In percent of exports)			Reserves (In months of imports)			Standard Deviation of Export Value		Reserves/Standard Deviation of Export Value	
		First export	Second export	Total	First export	Second export	Total	Pre-SAF or pre-ESAF	Most recent year	Change	Percent of exports	Months of imports	Pre-SAF or pre-ESAF	Most recent year
Bangladesh	Jute, ready-made garments	51	16	67	19	53	72	2.5	5.3	2.8	30.2	1.7	1.5	3.2
Bolivia[1]	Hydrocarbons, tin, zinc	57	18	75	32	18	50	8.4	4.6	−3.8	15.8	1.7	5.1	2.8
Burundi[2]	Coffee, manufactures, tea	84	5	89	80	9	89	1.4	5.2	3.8	18.4	1.3	1.1	4.2
Gambia, The[3,4]	Groundnuts, fish	82	11	93	65	17	82	0.2	4.9	4.7	24.1	2.2	0.1	2.2
Ghana	Cocoa, gold	67	14	81	36	30	66	2.2	4.2	2.0	16.6	1.7	1.3	2.5
Guinea[5]	Aluminum, diamonds	77	12	89	78	8	86	1.1	3.6	2.5	11.0	1.5	0.7	2.3
Guyana	Sugar, bauxite	42	36	78	38	37	75	0.9	6.0	5.2	7.3	0.8	1.1	7.4
Kenya	Coffee, tea	26	22	48	29	16	45	1.7	1.1	−0.6	13.9	0.9	1.9	1.3
Lesotho[6]	Clothing, cereals, livestock materials	27	20	47	67	6	73	1.2	1.9	0.7	25.5	0.3	4.3	7.0
Madagascar[4,7]	Vanilla, shellfish, coffee	44	16	60	17	11	28	4.6	2.6	−2.0	14.0	1.5	3.1	1.8
Malawi[4,8]	Tobacco, tea, sugar	62	11	73	62	12	74	1.8	3.4	1.6	20.1	1.8	1.0	1.9
Mauritania	Iron, fish	66	33	99	50	48	98	1.2	1.2	—	7.7	1.0	1.2	1.2
Mozambique[9]	Prawns, manufactures, cashews	48	22	70	37	23	60	1.6	3.7	2.1	24.0	0.4	3.6	8.3
Niger	Uranium, livestock products	77	9	86	66	20	86	5.5	6.5	1.0	15.1	1.5	3.6	4.3
Senegal[4]	Fish, groundnuts	29	12	41	25	19	44	—	0.1	—	8.1	0.7	0.1	0.1
Sri Lanka	Garments/textiles, tea	31	26	57	39	22	61	1.6	2.7	1.1	13.8	1.1	1.4	2.4
Tanzania	Coffee, manufactures	53	11	64	22	20	42	0.6	3.4	2.9	58.6	2.1	0.3	1.7
Togo[4,10]	Phosphates, cotton, coffee	49	13	62	49	25	74	7.3	6.3	−1.0	7.2	0.8	9.6	8.3
Uganda	Coffee, cotton	86	1	87	68	4	72	1.0	1.6	0.6	29.9	2.1	0.5	0.8
Mean		56	16	72	46	21	67	2.4	3.6	1.2	19.0	1.3	2.2	3.3

Source: IMF staff estimates.
[1] Zinc replaced tin as second most important export.
[2] Tea replaced manufactures as second most important export.
[3] Note significant unreported exports of groundnuts.
[4] Excludes re-exports and adjustments.
[5] Includes exports to the former U.S.S.R.
[6] Cereals replaced livestock materials as second most important export. In Lesotho workers' remittances exceed exports.
[7] Vanilla replaced coffee as the most important export.
[8] Tea replaced sugar as second most important export.
[9] Manufactures replaced cashews as second most important export.
[10] Cotton replaced coffee as second most important export.

Table 11. Indicators of Macroeconomic Performance by Country
(Annual averages, in percent, unless otherwise noted)

	Real GDP Growth			Export Volume Growth[1]			Import Volume Growth		
	Pre-SAF or pre-ESAF[2]	Latest three years[3]	Latest year	Pre-SAF or pre-ESAF[2]	Latest three years[3]	Latest year	Pre-SAF or pre-ESAF[2]	Latest three years[3]	Latest year
I. Countries that made relatively more progress toward external viability									
Bangladesh	4.2	4.1	3.2	5.0	12.6	13.9	5.9	−0.7	4.1
Bolivia	−1.1	3.2	4.1	0.6	14.3	−0.7	4.4	7.8	3.0
Gambia, The	−1.0	3.8	4.0	12.7	9.0	4.2	−9.1	9.6	4.0
Ghana	6.3	4.5	5.0	10.3	10.5	14.1	16.9	4.4	3.4
Guyana	−1.7	—	6.0	−8.5	—	17.5	−15.5	−2.1	−2.8
Lesotho[4]	1.4	2.5	0.3	15.0	−9.4	4.1	3.7	−2.6	−7.5
Malawi	2.0	5.6	7.8	−0.1	9.9	5.3	−0.7	16.7	19.9
Mozambique	−3.4	3.1	2.7	−19.0	15.2	25.0	−0.8	4.0	4.0
Senegal	0.8	2.4	2.3	−1.0	−0.8	−3.2	1.7	4.9	0.2
Sri Lanka	3.6	4.4	4.8	1.8	8.4	1.5	−2.0	7.1	15.5
Togo	2.7	1.5	—	6.5	−0.3	2.3	12.1	−1.1	−3.8
Mean	1.3	3.2	3.7	2.0	6.3	7.6	1.5	4.4	3.6
Median	1.4	3.2	4.0	1.8	9.0	4.1	1.8	4.4	2.2
II. Countries that made relatively little progress toward external viability									
Burundi	4.6	3.5	5.0	6.1	4.3	25.7	−5.1	4.4	9.0
Guinea	...	3.1	1.9	...	1.9	1.4	...	2.3	3.0
Kenya	5.5	4.0	2.4	2.6	0.5	−3.5	5.8	−5.4	−9.2
Madagascar	1.6	—	−6.9	−2.5	10.1	1.5	−8.4	4.3	−15.0
Mauritania	1.1	1.8	2.6	2.4	−3.6	−4.0	3.0	−1.0	−5.0
Niger	6.2	0.1	1.9	−4.9	0.2	4.1	−9.8	−8.3	−19.6
Tanzania	3.0	3.6	3.8	5.8	1.4	11.0	−2.0	−1.8	3.8
Uganda	0.8	4.7	4.2	...	1.2	7.9	...	−10.4	−26.6
Mean[6]	3.3	2.6	1.9	1.6	2.0	6.1	−2.7	−2.6	−8.9
Median[6]	3.0	3.5	2.5	2.5	1.3	4.1	−2.7	−1.0	−9.2

Source: IMF staff estimates.
[1]Merchandise only. These data differ from those in Table 6, which show the growth of exports of goods and nonfactor services.
[2]Average during three years preceding first SAF- or ESAF-supported program.
[3]Average during most recent three-year period ending in 1991 or 1991/92.
[4]Investment and saving computed as a ratio to GNP.
[5]Gross national savings, domestically generated for The Gambia, Lesotho, and Guinea.
[6]Excluding Guinea, for which data are not available for the three years before SAF/ESAF arrangements.

Link Between Domestic Performance and Progress Toward External Viability

Those countries that made the most progress in improving their debt position were also those that showed the strongest improvement in their domestic economic performance (Table 11). In almost all of the 11 countries where visible progress toward external viability occurred, the growth of *real GDP* rose considerably between the three years prior to the first SAF or ESAF program and the three most recent years; for the group, annual average GDP growth rose by almost 2 percentage points. Outside this group—that is, among countries where there was little or no progress toward external viability—the average annual growth rate fell by over half a percentage point during the same period.

A similar pattern is seen in the growth of *trade volumes*. The growth rates of both export and import volumes rose sharply in most of the countries where debt burdens were reduced. The contribution of strong export volume growth to the progress toward viability in most of these countries has already been emphasized. Stronger export growth, together with the greater availability of financing, also provided the scope for more rapid import growth—or in Guyana, a significantly less onerous contraction. In several countries, the growth in import

Inflation (CPI)			Investment (In percent of GDP)			Domestic Saving (In percent of GDP)		
Pre-SAF or pre-ESAF[2]	Latest three years[3]	Latest year	Pre-SAF or pre-ESAF[2]	Latest three years[3]	Latest year	Pre-SAF or pre-ESAF[2]	Latest three years[3]	Latest year
10.2	7.7	5.1	12.2	11.6	11.9	4.8[5]	3.2[5]	4.3[5]
664.0	17.9	21.4	8.5	12.8	13.8	4.5	7.3	7.5
23.9	10.3	11.5	19.8	19.6	19.0	2.1[5]	4.6[5]	5.1[5]
24.3	26.6	18.0	8.7	16.0	16.5	8.7[5]	12.3[5]	12.3[5]
50.6	85.6	105.9	24.4	26.6	25.4	11.5	17.5	17.4
12.3	15.1	15.5	24.5	48.0	58.9	18.2[5]	14.3[5]	17.6[5]
18.7	13.0	11.9	15.4	19.7	18.8	8.9	12.0	12.0
34.0	41.3	33.2	8.3	38.6	42.1	−0.6	−12.7	−10.0
11.6	1.0	2.1	14.8	13.5	13.5	2.6	8.6	8.5
5.7	15.0	12.2	23.6	22.3	23.0	14.5[5]	16.3[5]	17.5[5]
0.7	0.1	0.5	25.7	22.1	19.3	14.7	12.7	10.2
77.8	21.2	21.6	16.9	22.8	23.8	8.2	8.7	9.3
18.7	14.5	11.5	15.4	19.7	19.0	8.7	12.0	10.2
8.7	9.2	8.9	16.7	17.3	16.7	1.7	−0.6	−1.7
...	22.4	19.6	...	16.2	15.7	...	6.1[5]	5.3[5]
8.4	16.2	19.6	24.0	22.3	18.0	17.7[5]	18.0[5]	17.6[5]
12.5	9.8	8.5	8.7	12.9	8.2	4.0	6.3	1.5
9.8	8.3	5.6	23.9	18.2	16.1	6.1	8.8	8.2
−0.5	−0.3	1.3	14.3	10.8	7.2	7.0	7.3	7.5
32.9	21.6	21.0	...	...	...	...	...	...
179.3	39.8	63.0	2.7	12.0	13.0	—	−1.4	1.6
35.9	14.9	18.3	14.9	15.6	13.2	6.1	6.4	5.8
9.8	9.8	8.9	14.3	14.0	15.7	4.0	6.3	5.3

volumes in recent years followed a period of considerable import compression. By contrast, in the countries that made little or no progress toward external viability, export volume growth strengthened less; this, together with the generally weaker terms of trade in these countries, contributed to a considerable compression of imports in recent years.

Developments in consumer price *inflation* also differed between the two groups of countries: in the countries that made more progress toward viability, the median inflation rate fell by 7 percentage points between the three years preceding SAF/ESAF arrangements and the most recent year; in the other group it also fell but only slightly. However, even in the most recent year for which data are available, the median inflation rate in the countries that made the greatest progress toward viability was higher than in the other group.

Savings and investment data for the ESAF countries are weak at best, and wide differences in quality and coverage make cross-country comparisons hazardous. With this caveat, the picture that emerges is of increases in average and median investment ratios in the countries where the strongest progress toward external viability occurred; however, considerable variation across countries persisted. The average for the group was heavily influenced by Mozambique, where there was large investment to rebuild war-torn infrastructure, and Lesotho, where a large water project was undertaken. In five of the countries, the investment ratio actually fell. Developments in the group of countries that did not improve their debt positions were even less favorable. Except in Uganda, where there was an increase, each of the other countries saw little change or a decline in the investment ratio. In view of the fact that most of these countries experienced significant deteriorations in their terms of trade (which would raise investment ratios if volumes were constant), this picture is rather bleak. There was also a considerable difference in savings behavior. Whereas savings ratios rose slightly on average in the countries that made visible progress toward viability, they fell slightly in the countries that did not reduce their debt. These developments in investment and saving were reflected in a small increase in average current account deficits relative to GDP (Appendix Table A14).

Influences on Domestic Performance

These developments suggest that for most countries, progress in reducing the external debt burden and normalizing relations with creditors was generally reinforced by stronger growth of GDP and exports and lower inflation. The roles of policy adjustments, external factors, and other influences in these developments is not easy to sort out. There were numerous influences on the performance of

Table 12. Domestic Policy and External Developments
(Annual averages)

	Central Government Budget Deficit *(In percent of GDP)*			Real Effective Exchange Rate *(Average annual percent change)*			Growth of Broad Money *(Average annual percent change)*		
	Three years before SAF/ESAF	Year before SAF/ESAF	Most recent year	Three years before SAF/ESAF	SAF	ESAF	Three years before SAF/ESAF	SAF	ESAF
I. Countries that made relatively more progress toward external viability									
Bangladesh	−9.1	−7.5	−5.3	2.8	−3.2	−3.8	28.3	15.9	13.1
Bolivia	−20.5	−1.3	−1.8	−0.1	−3.6	−5.4	...	48.2	44.9
Gambia, The	−9.3	−1.5	0.9	9.4	−11.3	−1.8	19.8	32.2	11.7
Ghana	−1.8	0.1	1.6	−35.1	−22.9	−1.8	61.7	53.0	25.7
Guyana	−49.8	−48.4	−33.2	−14.6	...	−21.6	47.8	...	64.8
Lesotho	−6.2	−10.3	−0.6	−2.6	−1.1	2.0	16.8	20.0	1.1
Malawi	−7.8	−7.0	−3.0	−5.7	...	4.5	19.5	...	14.5
Mozambique	−18.1	−15.3	−6.0	30.7	−31.9	−8.6	15.4	50.7	33.9
Senegal	−4.6	−2.3	0.2	9.3	1.7	−4.5	3.0	9.3	2.7
Sri Lanka	−9.7	−8.7	−9.4	−9.3	−1.9	5.3	11.5	16.0	21.7
Togo	−1.6	−6.9	−5.9	6.8	3.0	8.9	7.7	−7.8	4.4
Median	−9.1	−7.0	−3.0	−0.1	−3.2	−1.8	19.6	20.5	14.5
Mean	−12.6	−9.9	−5.7	−0.8	−7.9	−2.4	23.1	26.4	19.4
II. Countries that made relatively little progress toward external viability									
Burundi	−15.2	−6.8	−4.0	2.1	−9.8	−6.4	15.9	7.2	3.4
Guinea	...	−5.5	−4.6	...	...	...	...	29.7	44.1
Kenya	−6.0	−2.9	−3.3	−7.2	−5.0	−3.9	16.7	8.3	19.0
Madagascar	−4.0	−3.5	−5.6	−5.5	−22.4	−3.9	18.3	18.9	18.5
Mauritania	−10.7	−2.4	−4.1	−7.8	−6.5	−1.2	14.0	9.6	12.4
Niger	−4.8	−3.6	−3.3	−5.5	−7.4	−7.0	4.9	8.7	6.4
Tanzania	−7.2	−2.6	1.5	−24.4	−33.2	−1.1	...	36.1	40.5
Uganda	−9.2	−4.0	−7.5	−45.9	−56.1	−36.4	176.7	165.0	55.6
Median	−7.2	−3.6	−4.1	−7.2	−9.8	−3.9	16.3[3]	9.2[3]	9.4
Mean	−8.2[4]	−3.9	−3.9	−13.5	−20.1	−8.6	41.1[3]	36.3[3]	19.2

Source: IMF staff estimates.
[1]One-year deposit rate deflated by increase in consumer prices.
[2]Defined as grants, loans, arrears, rescheduling, and IMF purchases less scheduled interest and amortization.
[3]Excluding Guinea and Tanzania.
[4]Excluding Guinea.

these economies, and many are not quantifiable. Structural reforms stand out in this respect: all of the countries under review implemented structural reforms in at least one key area, but comparing, let alone quantifying, these influences is not possible. Still, there is evidence that bold and comprehensive structural reforms have brought high returns: the four countries where reforms were most forceful—Bolivia, The Gambia, Ghana, and Guyana—were among the strongest performers of the countries under review (Box 4). Moreover, countries where there was less progress toward external viability tended to be those that had difficulties sustaining their structural reform programs. For some countries, reforms during SAF arrangements were considerably less forceful than during subsequent ESAF arrangements, and the latter are recent enough that their effects are not yet evident. In other countries, such as Madagascar and Niger, the process of transition to a more democratic system was accompanied by persistent difficulties with policy implementation.

The role of financial policies and external developments is easier to compare among countries (Table 12). Generally, the countries with the best external and domestic performance undertook stronger financial adjustment measures than those where progress toward external viability and domestic performance was weaker. However, except in the area of fiscal policy, differences were not great. Countries with stronger performance reduced deficits of the central government relative to GDP by some 4 percentage points, while the countries with weaker

Real Interest Rate[1] (In percent)		Terms of Trade (Average annual percent change)				Net Resource Transfer[2] (In percent of GDP)			
Year before SAF/ESAF	Most recent year	Three years before SAF/ESAF	SAF	ESAF	Most recent year	Three years before SAF/ESAF	SAF	ESAF	Most recent year
—	4	7.9	1.7	0.1	1.9	6.9	6.5	6.0	5.9
−16	4	−9.5	−10.9	−5.5	−7.9	2.2	2.0	3.8	4.2
−22	2	5.3	−1.0	−0.7	−0.2	−21.1	20.1	16.2	16.4
−10	9	12.3	−8.2	−9.7	−4.2	−4.0	5.0	7.7	10.1
−45	−29	−1.9	...	−2.7	−1.1	−6.1	...	37.6	14.0
−4	−1	...	...	...	...	19.9	23.9	26.5	19.3
1	1	−7.1	...	3.5	7.0	5.6	...	12.5	8.1
−56	−1	...	−4.9	−0.8	4.8	20.0	41.3	44.8	47.2
1	7	6.2	−0.9	3.9	3.7	18.7	28.0	23.1	23.2
—	5	−6.9	−2.7	2.7	2.7	2.7	4.0	7.7	7.7
5	6	−3.5	−1.6	−1.0	1.3	21.2	27.1	32.1	24.0
−4	4	−1.9	−2.2	−0.8	1.6	6.9	20.1	16.2	14.0
−13	1	0.3	−3.6	−1.0	0.8	10.6	17.5	19.8	16.4
3	1	13.0	−5.1	−11.1	5.8	14.8	18.4	20.9	20.9
−30	7	−12.1	−3.4	−2.6	−2.6	5.5	6.4	5.8	5.8
—	4	−6.2	2.1	−5.2	5.7	−0.6	7.0	3.6	0.5
1	2	2.3	−15.6	−9.6	−3.4	12.2	20.4	17.3	13.9
1	3	9.1	−6.3	0.5	8.1	21.4	20.3	20.0	10.5
11	6	−2.2	−4.9	−8.9	−7.3	22.2	22.6	24.7	12.6
−15	1	−2.1	−5.1	−5.6	−5.6	29.3	19.5	19.8	19.8
−61	6	...	−25.0	−17.4	−14.2	−0.3	11.1	11.6	9.3
1	3.5	−2.1	−5.1	−7.3	−3.0	13.5	19.0	18.7	11.6
−11	4.0	0.3	−7.9	−7.5	−1.7	13.1	15.7	15.5	11.7

performances held fiscal deficits steady relative to GDP. In contrast, money growth rates tended to be higher and to fall by less during the SAF/ESAF period in the countries that achieved the greatest improvements in domestic and external performance; interest rates rose by about the same amount in both groups of countries. Countries that progressed less toward external viability experienced larger real depreciations than the others; this difference reflected efforts to address the relatively large terms of trade shocks in these countries. It is notable that in most respects, financial policies prior to the SAF/ESAF period were weaker in the first group of countries than in the second group; the stronger adjustment of fiscal deficits in the first group left average fiscal deficits, money growth, and real interest rates broadly the same in the two groups of countries.

The striking difference between the two groups is in external developments. The deterioration in the terms of trade in the countries with weaker performance was a large multiple of that in the countries with stronger performances. Uganda is noteworthy in this respect: notwithstanding considerable structural change, external indicators weakened sharply, principally on account of the exceptionally large deterioration in the terms of trade. Net resource transfers, while lower relative to GDP in the weaker performers, differed considerably less. These comparisons point to the large role that the terms of trade played both in supporting (or not undercutting) the good policies of the strong performers, and in offsetting the effects of broadly stable financial policies in the countries with relatively weak domestic and external performance. Moreover, the fact that several of the countries with relatively weak financial policies also experienced large deteriorations in their terms of trade may well reflect the difficulty of reining in fiscal deficits and money growth in the face of adverse terms of trade developments.

Box 4. Successful Adjustment—Bolivia, The Gambia, Ghana, and Guyana

The benefits of financial adjustment and structural reform are perhaps most striking in four countries—Bolivia, The Gambia, Ghana, and Guyana—where strong measures across a broad spectrum of issues were implemented in the course of previous stand-by arrangements (for Bolivia and Ghana) and the SAF and ESAF arrangements. Starting from among the most distorted positions and weakest performances in the group of countries under consideration, these four countries sharply reduced central government budget deficits and fundamentally revised the role of the public sector in public enterprises, marketing boards, price policies, the allocation of foreign exchange, and the setting of the exchange rate. The results were dramatic: a declining trend in per capita GDP was reversed, exports surged, and (except in Ghana) inflation was sharply reduced. In Bolivia and Ghana, strong domestic economic performance was sustained through the SAF/ESAF period despite a sharp deterioration in the terms of trade that precluded progress in reducing the debt ratio in Ghana. In the other three countries, the ratio of debt to exports fell, while in The Gambia timely payments of contractual debt-service obligations were restored.

V Summary of Findings and Conclusions

The countries undertaking ESAF arrangements faced daunting obstacles. They had among the lowest per capita income levels in the world and weak foundations for growth—inadequate economic infrastructure and underdeveloped human capital. Distortions and rigidities stemming from official controls and poorly designed tax and expenditure policies perpetuated economic weakness and drove the financial and external imbalances that had given rise to unsustainable debt burdens.

The ESAF presented a channel for IMF involvement in these low-income countries, tailored to their needs by two distinguishing characteristics. First, ESAF programs took a medium-term perspective on the interaction between macroeconomic policies and structural reform—a perspective that has benefited from the collaboration between the World Bank and the IMF in designing structural policies. Thus, the ESAF permitted the IMF to support not just macroeconomic and financial stabilization, but also reforms to address the structural weaknesses that were at the root of financial instability and excessive external debt burdens. The second distinguishing characteristic was that the concessional nature of ESAF resources enabled these countries, which in general can ill afford to borrow on market-related terms, to enter into IMF-supported programs.

The performance of countries under the ESAF arrangements must be judged against the extraordinarily weak starting positions and, for many, serious deteriorations in the external terms of trade during the arrangements. Against this backdrop, the experience under ESAF arrangements has in general been favorable. While there remains considerable room for improvement, the ESAF countries have on average seen a strengthening in a wide range of macroeconomic indicators—real GDP growth, trade volumes, inflation, and debt ratios. There have been disappointments, particularly in the relatively small response of investment ratios and the persistence of low savings ratios. The review of individual countries' experiences suggests that the largest improvements in macroeconomic performance occurred in countries that undertook the most forceful reforms and suffered the least from weakening terms of trade.

The 19 countries under review made sustained policy changes in at least one—and in several countries, many—important areas. Generally, fiscal adjustment was not as forceful as structural reform. Most countries reduced the deficit of the central government relative to GDP, but the average reduction was modest—about 2 percentage points. Several developments thwarted stronger adjustment. For one thing, several countries had reduced central government deficits in the two or three years before the SAF/ESAF period, and further reductions required especially difficult policy measures. In some countries, such structural reforms as increases in interest rates and other financial sector measures put upward pressure on deficits. In a small number there were simply slippages in the implementation of expenditure control and revenue-raising efforts. In almost all countries, available indicators point to an overall public sector deficit that was substantially higher than the narrowly defined deficit of the central government.

For many countries, structural reforms, even if not comprehensive, resulted in important changes in the role of the government. The breadth and depth of reform, however, varied considerably. Changes were most pronounced in three areas: exchange and trade liberalization, decontrol of agricultural prices and marketing boards, and liberalization of interest rates. In other areas, actions were less forceful; in particular, much remains to be done in the areas of bank restructuring and public enterprise reform. Continuing weaknesses in these areas are interrelated. Coordinated action to address them will be crucial to the improvements in economic efficiency and financial balances needed to sustain newly liberalized exchange, trade, and pricing regimes.

In many of the 19 ESAF countries under review, currency depreciation was an important component of efforts to support exchange and trade reform, to correct initial overvaluation, and to respond to terms of trade losses.[19] For most countries real de-

[19]In Lesotho and the member countries of the West African Monetary Union, currency depreciation was ruled out by adherence to fixed exchange rate regimes.

preciations, although smaller than the nominal changes, were sizable and strongly influenced export growth. In general, the rate of nominal depreciation slowed in the most recent two to three years, resulting in a slower rate of real depreciation despite some reduction in inflation. For the future, lowering financial imbalances, particularly in the public sector, will be critical to maintaining, or, in some countries, strengthening, present levels of competitiveness.

A number of influences appear to have affected the forcefulness of reform and adjustment. First, the degree of political commitment to changing the role of the public sector was critical. This is manifest in the fact that countries where reforms in any one area were the strongest and the best sustained tended to be those that acted aggressively in a number of areas. Second, even with considerable technical assistance from the IMF and other institutions, limited administrative capacity to design and implement reforms was a constraint. In many countries, an important dimension of this problem was a bloated but underpaid and demoralized civil service. Third, political instability slowed or even reversed reforms in several countries. Fourth, declining terms of trade—especially from falling export prices—tended to inhibit action.

Progress toward external viability varied considerably. Almost all the countries under review entered the SAF/ESAF period with rising debt and debt-service ratios; about two-thirds had such heavy debt burdens that debt-service obligations were not being fully met. Almost all of them were able to halt the deterioration in their debt profiles during the program period. About half can be considered to have made progress toward viability in the sense of cutting or holding constant their debt and debt-service burdens and reducing or maintaining at a low level their reliance on exceptional financing. For several countries in this group, an end to the need for exceptional financing appears to be in prospect, although continued heavy reliance on foreign assistance in other forms is likely to be needed for some years to come. The other half of the countries under review experienced little change or even increases in debt and debt-service ratios and had increased recourse to exceptional financing.

There was a positive correlation between progress toward external viability and domestic economic performance. The countries that made more visible progress toward viability also saw average GDP growth rates, export and import volume growth rates, and savings ratios improve by significantly more than the countries where little or no progress toward external viability occurred. The two key factors for the more successful group were the forcefulness of structural reform—and to a lesser extent of financial adjustment—and developments in the terms of trade. In the group that made less progress toward external viability, several factors were at play: large deteriorations in the terms of trade that at times offset the benefits of structural reforms; political instability that caused disruptions to reform programs; and lack of political commitment to reform.

The sharp deterioration in the terms of trade in several ESAF countries raises questions about the balance between adjustment and financing. Most of the countries where the terms of trade fell made relatively little progress toward viability despite, in some cases, strong adjustment efforts; several experienced large increases in debt burdens, because they continued to borrow as nominal exports fell. Two lessons emerge from the experience of these countries. First, as the terms of trade deteriorate, the strength of adjustment needs to be reevaluated quickly. Second, financing for countries in such circumstances should be on highly concessional terms, particularly when there is no strong reason to believe the deterioration will be reversed soon.

SAF- and ESAF-supported programs paid increasing attention to poverty and the social costs of adjustment. While the most important developments for poverty alleviation were rising GDP growth and falling inflation, efforts were also made to improve social programs and infrastructure, increase public works employment, or provide transfers to the poor. Financing, administrative, and logistical constraints were a problem, but in general the efforts were judged successful, if modest in scale. Environmental considerations began to come into play in ESAF-supported programs but demand greater attention.

In most of the countries covered by this review, structural reform remains incomplete and external viability elusive, at least for the near term. Experience under the ESAF suggests several areas where the IMF should continue to play a role. First, firm discipline in financial policies is crucial. Despite continuous efforts to rein in fiscal deficits and credit expansion during SAF/ESAF arrangements, there is still room for improvement. Since continuing inflation undermines the response of savings and investment to structural reform, it will be critical in the coming years to bring it under control. Second, frameworks for coordinating domestic financial policies, structural reforms, and external financing will continue to be needed. For many countries, debt and debt service remain so high that even the strongest domestic policy efforts would be insufficient to restore external viability in the foreseeable future; substantial concessional financing including, for many countries, debt reduction will be necessary, but should be contingent on assurances that domestic adjustment and reform efforts are effective, sustained, and strong enough to prevent the reemergence of debt-servicing problems. Finally, administrative capacity remains a severe constraint in most countries, and well-targeted technical assistance from the IMF, the World Bank, and other institutions will be necessary.

Statistical Appendix

Table A1. Basic Indicators Prior to SAF/ESAF Period

(Annual average during the three years preceding first SAF- or ESAF-supported program unless otherwise noted)

	Summary Indicators (Percent change)							Financial Flows (In percent of GDP)				External Sector (In percent of exports except Reserves column)				
	Population growth (1980–90)	GDP growth	Export volume growth	Import volume growth	Inflation (CPI)	Terms of trade	Real effective exchange rate	Investment	Saving	External current account[1]	Fiscal balance[1]	External debt[2]	Debt service	Contractual less actual debt service	Official inflows[3]	Reserves[4]
Bangladesh	2.3	4.2	5.0	5.9	10.2	5.2	−1.3	12.2	4.8	−7.3	−8.0	492.8	27.4	—	101.4	2.5
Bolivia	2.5	−1.1	0.6	4.4	664.0	−10.0	−16.8	8.5	4.5	−7.6	−11.5	522.9	84.3	58.1	66.0	8.4
Burundi	2.8	4.6	6.1	−5.1	8.7	11.0	1.8	16.7	1.7	−15.4	−14.1	351.6	18.7	—	163.0	1.4
Gambia, The	3.4	−1.0	12.7	−9.1	23.9	−1.8	−1.2	19.8	16.3	−17.6	−11.8	373.1	8.4	23.7	61.2	0.2
Ghana	3.4	6.3	10.3	16.9	24.3	11.4	−45.1	8.7	8.7	−3.5	−4.3	331.2	45.6	−13.2	85.1	2.2
Guinea[5]	2.4	...	...	...	...	...	...	14.1	11.4	−5.6	−7.4	305.3	27.6	3.6	74.8	1.1
Guyana	−0.1	−1.7	−8.5	−15.5	50.6	−2.0	−20.1	24.4	11.5	−31.4	−47.3	903.4	106.8	72.2	101.4	0.9
Kenya	3.8	5.5	2.6	5.8	8.4	−7.4	−7.0	24.0	17.7	−4.6	−6.6	239.2	30.2	—	28.3	1.7
Lesotho	2.7	1.4	15.0	3.7	12.3	...	−2.0	24.5	23.5	−17.3	−14.3	51.6	4.7	—	35.6	1.2
Madagascar	3.0	1.6	−2.5	−8.4	12.5	1.3	−6.5	8.7	−0.9	−8.9	−4.4	663.7	71.5	47.8	122.3	4.6
Malawi	3.4	2.0	−0.1	−0.7	18.7	−7.2	−5.9	15.4	8.9	−6.3	−10.8	345.0	32.7	5.9	49.4	1.8
Mauritania	2.4	1.1	2.4	3.0	9.8	9.1	−7.2	23.9	6.1	−31.5	−8.3	327.9	38.3	14.8	80.6	1.2
Mozambique	2.6	−3.4	−19.0	−0.8	34.0	10.0	24.3	8.3	−0.6	−15.3	...	1,815.6	291.3	278.3	380.4	1.6
Niger	3.3	6.2	−4.9	−9.8	−0.5	−2.6	−4.2	14.3	7.0	−11.3	−9.3	294.6	51.2	17.1	101.1	5.5
Senegal	2.9	0.8	−2.3	1.7	11.6	6.1	6.3	14.8	2.6	−15.5	−4.8	270.7	26.0	8.9	53.7	—
Sri Lanka	1.4	3.6	1.8	−2.0	5.7	−7.5	−12.7	23.6	14.5	−9.1	−11.7	224.8	26.6	—	24.4	1.6
Tanzania	3.1	3.5	5.8	−2.0	32.9	−15.5	−38.5	22.5	...	...	−8.0	567.6	59.6	35.4	208.6	0.6
Togo	3.5	2.7	6.5	12.1	0.7	−3.6	1.0	25.7	14.7	−13.4	−8.0	211.7	30.0	9.4	39.8	7.3
Uganda	2.5	0.8	...	...	179.3	—	19.5	2.7	—	−3.6	−6.4	272.5	44.1	0.5	49.4	1.0
Mean	2.7	2.1	1.9	—	61.5	−0.2	−6.4	16.5	8.5	−12.5	−10.9	450.8	53.9	29.6	96.1	2.4
Median	2.8	1.8	2.4	−0.7	12.4	−0.6	−5.1	15.4	7.9	−10.2	−8.2	331.2	32.7	8.9	74.8	1.6

Sources: World Bank, *World Development Report*, various issues; and IMF staff estimates.

[1]Excludes official transfers. Fiscal balance is for central government only.

[2]Medium- and long-term external public debt at end of the year preceding the first SAF/ESAF arrangement.

[3]Disbursements of official loans and grants, including rescheduling and use of IMF resources.

[4]Reserves in months of imports during the year prior to the first SAF- or ESAF-supported program.

[5]Data available only for year immediately preceding SAF.

Table A2. Fiscal and Monetary Indicators Prior to SAF/ESAF Period

(Annual averages during the three years preceding first SAF- or ESAF-supported program)

	Central Government Budget (In percent of GDP)						Monetary Survey					Inflation and Interest Rates	
			Expenditures				Net domestic assets	Broad money	Net domestic assets	Net credit to public sector[2]	Broad money		
	Revenues[1]	Taxes	Total	Current	Capital	Overall balance[1]	(Annual change in percent of GDP)		(Annual change in percent of initial stock of broad money)			CPI (In percent)	Real interest rate[3] (In percent)
Bangladesh	8.7	7.0	16.7	7.6	8.1	−8.0	4.7	5.2	25.2	7.3	28.3	10.2	4.6
Bolivia	10.1	3.4	21.3	19.7	1.6	−11.2	12.8	8.7	...	...	...	664.0	13.2
Burundi	16.9	12.5	27.3	11.6	15.7	−10.4	1.8	2.3	12.3	10.8	15.9	8.7	6.0
Gambia, The	24.3	11.7	31.8	20.0	11.4	−7.1	9.4	3.7	42.3	20.5	19.8	23.9	−21.5
Ghana	12.4	9.4	15.2	10.6	4.7	−2.9	6.4	5.9	70.4	30.5	61.7	24.3	−8.7
Guinea[4]	15.0	1.5	20.5	13.0	7.5	−5.5	5.2	3.0	40.7	−0.4	89.7	28.3	−31.4
Guyana	39.4	33.5	84.5	70.7	14.2	−45.1	36.6	36.5	48.1	47.4	47.8	50.6	−43.8
Kenya	24.1	20.1	29.3	22.6	6.7	−5.2	5.0	4.3	19.3	13.2	16.7	8.4	3.6
Lesotho	23.2	16.7	33.5	19.4	14.1	−10.3	4.7	1.2	75.8	63.8	21.5	12.3	1.2
Madagascar	14.6	10.3	18.4	12.0	6.5	−3.8	4.5	3.1	27.8	0.4	18.3	12.5	−1.5
Malawi	24.0	16.7	31.8	22.8	7.7	−8.2	2.3	3.2	16.5	20.8	19.5	18.7	4.1
Mauritania	28.5	19.4	32.3	...	...	−5.9	4.6	3.0	22.9	−3.8	14.0	9.8	3.9
Mozambique	18.0	11.2	33.1	24.6	8.5	−15.1	8.8	9.3	14.4	26.3	15.4	34.0	−54.4
Niger	16.3	9.0	20.5	11.4	9.3	−4.2	−1.0	0.5	−5.6	0.8	4.9	−0.5	15.2
Senegal	19.9	16.8	23.4	19.6	3.3	−3.5	2.7	0.7	11.0	6.3	3.0	11.6	6.4
Sri Lanka	23.6	18.0	33.2	20.2	12.1	−9.5	4.1	3.5	13.6	7.3	11.5	5.7	7.3
Tanzania	18.0	15.1	24.0	18.7	5.3	−6.0	...	...	...	...	...	32.9	−11.0
Togo	31.0	21.3	35.4	23.0	12.0	−4.3	4.2	3.4	9.5	2.3	7.7	0.7	13.5
Uganda	6.3	5.3	12.0	8.6	3.4	−5.7	28.0	12.2	356.1	82.5	176.7	179.3	−58.5
Mean	19.7	13.6	28.6	19.8	8.5	−9.0	8.1	6.1	47.1	19.8	31.8	59.8	...
Median	18.0	12.5	27.3	19.5	7.9	−6.0	4.7	3.5	24.1	9.1	18.9	12.5	...

Source: IMF staff estimates.

[1]Including grants.

[2]Domestic banking system credit to government and nonfinancial public enterprises.

[3]Commercial bank loan rate during pre-SAF year deflated by the CPI inflation of the same year. The loan rate is either a weighted average or the midpoint in the range of loan rates.

[4]Data exist only for one pre-SAF year.

Table A3. Price Controls, Marketing Boards, and Trade Monopolies Prior to SAF/ESAF Period

	State-Controlled Exports[1] *(In percent of exports)*	State Involvement in Imports and Nontraded Goods[2]
Bangladesh	Jute (51%)	Fertilizer subsidized. Food grains subsidized.
Bolivia	None (0%)	Petroleum price set below world market price.
Burundi	Coffee (84%)	Retail prices administered.
Gambia, The	Groundnuts (82%)	Monopoly for rice imports. Fertilizer, agricultural inputs subsidized. Petroleum, electricity prices administered.
Ghana	Cocoa (67%)	Some prices controlled.
Guinea	Coffee, palm oil (4%)	Petroleum product prices controlled. Rice producer price set as a reference price.
Guyana	Sugar, rice (45%)	Prices of petroleum products, transportation, margarine, and powdered milk controlled.
Kenya	Grains, coffee, tea (48%)	Cereals, dairy, and meat under marketing boards. Extensive price controls.
Lesotho	None (0%)	Producer prices for five main foodcrops set by marketing board.
Madagascar	Cloves, coffee, vanilla, pepper (73%)	Price and profit margin ceilings set for ten commodities.
Malawi	Tobacco, cotton, groundnuts (64%)	Fertilizer subsidized. Maize, rice under marketing board. Prices of sugar, petrol products, low-grade meat, and spare parts controlled.
Mauritania	None (0%)	Petroleum products set low. Cereals, rice, tea, and sugar imported by marketing board.
Mozambique	All (100%)	State administered price system. Producer prices set low.
Niger	None (0%)	Cereals marketing board pricing by tender. Monopoly for petroleum imports. Profit margin ceilings set on 64 imports. Price ceilings on flour, petroleum, bread, salt, water, electricity, and transportation.
Senegal	Groundnuts, cotton (12%)	Prices set for petroleum products. Producer prices set for rice and other cereals. Sugar subsidized.
Sri Lanka	Tea, rubber (33%)	Petroleum, fertilizer, wheat, and some agricultural products monopolized.
Tanzania	Coffee, cotton, sisal, tea (70%)	Prices of fertilizer and other imported agricultural inputs controlled. Prices of 47 foods and consumer goods controlled.
Togo	Cocoa, coffee, cotton (30%)	Food grain producer prices set.
Uganda	Tea, cotton, coffee, tobacco (86%)	Petroleum products subsidized. Foodstuffs under produce marketing board.

[1]Commodities exported by state monopoly that sets producer prices.
[2]State involvement in setting producer or consumer prices via state trading companies and price controls.

Table A4. Exchange and Trade System Prior to First SAF or ESAF Arrangement
(In percent unless otherwise noted)

Country (Year)[1]	Parallel Market Premium	External Sector Performance		Significant Features of Exchange and Trade System
		Export volume[2]	Import volume[2]	
I. Countries with comprehensive restrictions on current transactions				
Guyana (1989)	100–300	−8.5	−14.0	Basket peg. Export retention—bauxite 100%, sugar 15%, others 10%. Import prohibitions. Licensing subject to foreign exchange availability. Sugar and bauxite monopolies.
Madagascar (1986)	...	−2.5	−7.9	Basket peg. Comprehensive trade and payment restrictions. Export surrender. State-managed imports. Import monopoly for rice, wheat, and alcohol.
Mauritania (1986)	140–170	3.7	−3.9	Managed exchange rate. Export surrender. Import licensing. All imports approved by central bank. Iron ore export monopoly. Sugar, rice, and tea import monopolies.
Mozambique (1986)	2,500–4,000	−19.0	−1.7	Basket peg. Comprehensive restrictions. Limited export retention. Foreign exchange allocated administratively. Imports and exports licensed within foreign exchange budget.
Tanzania (1986)	200	−1.6	8.0	Basket peg. Export retention of 10%–50%. Extensive licensing of imports and exports.
Uganda (1986)	...	−4.7	7.3	Peg to U.S. dollar. Comprehensive foreign exchange allocation through monthly foreign exchange budget. Export surrender. Export monopolies for main agricultural exports.
II. Countries with some restrictions on current transactions				
Bangladesh (1985)	9.5	5.0	5.9	Basket peg. Secondary foreign exchange market with 54% premium, handles 43% of export receipts. Comprehensive trade restrictions.
Burundi (1985)	...	6.1	−5.1	SDR peg. Coffee export monopoly. Export surrender. Import licenses require central bank approval—denied for many goods.
Ghana (1986)	100	11.0	16.2	Dual rate. Cocoa receipts go to official market for government use. Other exports surrendered at weekly auction rate, available for imports or producer goods. Export retention 20%. Cocoa export monopoly.
Guinea (1986)	20	...	...	Dual rate including auction. No licensing but prior authorization for foreign exchange allocation. Mining sector imports outside auction system.
Kenya (1987)	90–100	2.6	5.8	Basket peg. Extensive quotas. Exchange allocation licenses. Coffee export monopoly. Export surrender.
Malawi (1987)	...	−0.1	−1.2	Basket peg. Foreign exchange surrender. Foreign exchange allocated by central bank with reference to a foreign exchange budget.
Sri Lanka (1987)	...	1.8	−2.0	Adjustable peg. Import licenses for specified commodities including major food grains. Export quotas. Foreign exchange restriction on travel only.
III. Countries with no major restrictions on current transactions				
Bolivia (1986)	1.3	5.3	−1.9	Auction market. Few remaining restrictions. Uniform tariff of 20%.
Gambia, The (As of January 1986)	3	−12.5	−3.7	Floating interbank market. Open general license. Export monopolies on groundnuts, palm kernels, and cotton. Uniform 5% import tax.
Lesotho (1987)	0	15.0	3.7	Common monetary area and customs union.
Niger (1986)	0	−5.7	−9.4	CFA zone. Prior authorization for import of rice, sugar, wheat flour, some textiles.
Senegal (1985)	0	−1.0	1.8	CFA zone. Some quantitative restrictions.
Togo (1987)	0	4.1	11.6	CFA zone. Export monopolies for phosphates and main agricultural exports. Import licenses, liberally administered, permit access to foreign exchange.

Sources: International Monetary Fund, *Annual Report on Exchange Arrangements and Exchange Restrictions* (Washington, International Monetary Fund), various issues.
[1]Exchange restrictions at end-December of the indicated year except for The Gambia.
[2]Average growth rates during three years preceding first SAF- or ESAF-supported program.

Table A5. Terms of Trade Developments During SAF/ESAF Period[1]

(Annual average percent change)

	Export Unit Value	Import Unit Value	Terms of Trade
Uganda	−19.6	2.2	−21.3
Madagascar (SDR)	−10.4	2.1	−12.2
Burundi	−5.2	4.9	−9.6
Ghana	−4.0	6.1	−9.5
Niger (CFA)	−6.0	1.6	−7.4
Bolivia	−3.5	3.7	−6.8
Tanzania	−0.9	4.6	−5.3
Mozambique	1.1	5.5	−4.2
Kenya (SDR)	−0.6	3.2	−3.6
Guinea	1.0	4.7	−3.5
Guyana	4.3	7.2	−2.7
Mauritania (SDR)	0.2	2.8	−2.5
Sri Lanka	1.9	3.1	−1.4
Togo (CFA)	1.1	2.3	−1.2
Gambia, The (SDR)	2.9	3.7	−0.8
Malawi (SDR)	5.7	4.7	1.0
Bangladesh	3.3	2.3	1.0
Senegal (CFA)	1.4	−0.6	2.1
Minimum	−19.6	−0.6	−21.3
Maximum	5.7	7.2	2.1
Average (arithmetic)	−1.5	3.5	−4.9
Countries that experienced large TOT deterioration prior to programs[2]	1.7	3.8	−2.1
Countries that experienced large TOT deterioration during programs[3]	−4.7	4.1	−8.4

Source: IMF staff estimates.

[1]Import and export price changes measured in U.S. dollars unless another currency indicated in parentheses. Lesotho is excluded from the table because reliable data were not available.

[2]The Gambia, Togo, Sri Lanka, Malawi, Kenya, and Tanzania.

[3]Guinea, Mozambique, Burundi, Tanzania, Ghana, Kenya, Uganda, Madagascar, and Bolivia.

Table A6. Export Prices of Key Commodities in SAF/ESAF Countries
(Annual percent change in U.S. dollars unless otherwise noted)

Commodity	Exporting Countries	1986	1987	1988	1989	1990	1991	Cumulative Change During 1985–91
Bauxite	Guinea, Guyana	−4.9	7.0	−0.3	−14.7	0.9	10.9	−3.2
Cashew	Mozambique	44.8	−6.4	−22.7	−14.0	−5.7	35.8	15.4
Cloves[1]	Madagascar	−7.2	16.6	−22.2	−11.9	1.2	−13.1	−34.8
Cocoa	Ghana	−8.3	−3.4	−20.7	−21.6	2.1	−5.9	−47.1
Coffee	Madagascar, Burundi, Kenya, Tanzania, Uganda	22.3	−31.1	−6.9	−20.0	−27.6	−9.1	−58.7
Cotton	Burundi, Tanzania, Togo	−20.0	56.2	−15.1	19.5	8.8	−6.9	28.4
Fish	Mauritania, Senegal	14.6	19.3	42.0	−24.8	0.7	16.0	70.5
Garments	Bangladesh, Lesotho, Sri Lanka	12.0	15.6	2.1	−2.1	7.2	10.2	52.9
Gold	Ghana	15.9	21.4	−2.1	−12.8	0.6	−5.6	14.1
Groundnuts	Gambia, Senegal	−37.1	−12.1	18.2	31.1	24.4	−7.2	−1.1
Iron ore	Mauritania	−3.5	1.4	5.9	12.8	16.2	8.1	46.8
Jute	Bangladesh	−53.3	18.0	15.2	0.8	9.4	−7.4	−35.1
Livestock	Niger	−3.1	13.7	5.6	1.8	—	4.3	23.5
Manufactured products	Mozambique	17.7	11.9	6.0	−0.9	9.3	1.9	54.1
Petroleum	Bolivia, Kenya	−48.8	28.7	−20.5	21.5	28.3	−17.0	−32.2
Phosphates	Togo	1.2	−9.6	16.1	13.3	−0.7	4.9	25.4
Prawns	Mozambique	14.8	11.1	13.1	−10.2	3.2	−6.4	25.1
Sugar	Guyana	48.8	11.5	50.0	25.5	−2.3	−28.0	119.7
Tea	Burundi, Malawi, Sri Lanka	−2.5	−11.4	4.7	12.3	1.0	−9.4	−7.1
Tin	Bolivia	−43.8	7.5	4.7	19.3	−28.9	−9.6	−51.5
Tobacco	Malawi, Tanzania	−10.9	−4.3	3.8	6.7	2.3	3.9	0.4
Uranium	Niger	29.7	12.5	−4.9	−15.3	−4.5	−11.9	−1.1
Vanilla	Madagascar	—	1.69	−1.0	1.4	2.0	−0.1	4.1
Wool	Lesotho	−6.0	53.0	63.4	−20.4	−12.8	−31.2	12.2

Source: IMF staff estimates.
[1]Includes essence of cloves.

Table A7. Net Resource Transfer During SAF/ESAF Period[1]

	Official Loans			Official Transfers			Actual Debt-Service Payments			Total Net Resource Transfer		
	Year before SAF	Year before ESAF	Latest year[2]	Year before SAF	Year before ESAF	Latest year[2]	Year before SAF	Year before ESAF	Latest year[2]	Year before SAF	Year before ESAF	Latest year[2]
	(In millions of U.S. dollars)											
Bangladesh	871	1,110	1,194	546	725	670	470	551	510	947	1,284	1,354
Bolivia	370	212	331	82	103	160	239	231	280	213	85	211
Burundi	74	88	88	79	164	182	29	39	35	123	213	235
Gambia, The	7	29	32	34	49	49	1	38	26	40	39	55
Ghana	401	562	634	118	122	222	367	562	324	153	122	532
Guinea	144	194	227	42	101	110	79	125	152	108	170	184
Guyana	...	7	47	...	67	78	...	71	92	...	3	33
Kenya	525	771	561	142	257	204	608	586	720	59	442	45
Lesotho	27	66	79	91	174	154	10	13	16	108	228	218
Madagascar	244	209	189	110	125	113	90	158	105	264	175	197
Malawi	...	123	171	...	35	185	...	118	106	...	40	251
Mauritania	161	121	73	107	92	81	119	86	35	149	127	120
Mozambique	259	225	186	173	475	502	19	52	19	413	648	669
Niger	121	96	20	148	137	139	120	85	75	149	148	84
Senegal	228	507	331	134	209	228	195	325	174	167	391	385
Sri Lanka	490	408	579	180	176	203	517	451	491	153	133	291
Tanzania	243	252	211	363	530	549	25	151	148	581	631	612
Togo	81	121	70	97	75	87	48	85	32	129	111	125
Uganda	220	321	447	40	131	217	171	166	125	89	286	539
Total	4,465	5,424	5,470	2,488	3,747	4,133	3,106	3,893	3,463	3,847	5,277	6,139
Average	263	285	288	146	197	218	183	205	182	226	278	323

Table A7 (continued)

	Official Loans			Official Transfers			Actual Debt-Service Payments			Total Net Resource Transfer		
	Year before SAF	Year before ESAF	Latest year[2]	Year before SAF	Year before ESAF	Latest year[2]	Year before SAF	Year before ESAF	Latest year[2]	Year before SAF	Year before ESAF	Latest year[2]
						(In percent of GDP)						
Bangladesh	6	5	5	3	3	3	3	2	2	6	6	6
Bolivia	10	5	7	2	2	3	6	5	6	5	2	4
Burundi	6	8	7	7	15	15	3	4	3	11	19	20
Gambia, The	4	12	10	17	21	15	1	16	8	20	17	16
Ghana	7	12	10	2	3	3	6	12	5	3	3	8
Guinea	7	6	7	2	3	3	4	4	5	6	6	6
Guyana	...	3	20	...	24	33	...	26	39	...	1	14
Kenya	7	9	7	2	3	2	8	7	9	1	5	1
Lesotho	4	6	7	12	17	14	1	1	1	14	22	19
Madagascar	7	9	7	3	5	4	3	6	4	8	7	7
Malawi	...	9	8	...	2	9	...	8	5	...	3	12
Mauritania	19	13	6	13	10	7	14	9	3	18	13	10
Mozambique	8	17	14	5	37	38	1	4	1	12	50	51
Niger	6	4	1	8	6	6	6	4	3	8	6	4
Senegal	8	11	6	5	4	4	7	7	3	6	8	7
Sri Lanka	10	7	9	3	3	3	10	8	7	3	2	4
Tanzania	6	9	7	9	18	18	1	5	5	14	22	20
Togo	6	9	4	8	5	5	4	6	2	10	8	8
Uganda	4	7	14	1	3	7	3	3	4	2	6	17

Source: IMF staff estimates.
[1]Defined as all official loans and grants plus IMF purchases less actual debt-service payments made.
[2]Calendar year 1991 or fiscal year 1991/92.

Table A8. Official Multilateral Debt Reschedulings for SAF/ESAF Countries

	Date of Agreement	Consolidation Period *(In months)*	Terms Under Which Debt Rescheduled		
			Standard terms	Toronto terms	Enhanced concessions
Bolivia	July 7, 1986	12	*		
	Nov. 14, 1988	15	*		
	Mar. 15, 1990	24		*	
	Jan. 24, 1992	18			*
Gambia, The	Sep. 19, 1986	12	*		
Guinea	Apr. 18, 1986	14	*		
	Apr. 12, 1989	12		*	
	Nov. 18, 1992	12			*
Guyana	May 24, 1989	14	*		
	Sep. 12, 1990	35		*	
Madagascar	Oct. 23, 1986	21	*		
	Oct. 28, 1988	21		*	
	July 10, 1990	13		*	
Malawi	Apr. 22, 1988	14	*		
Mauritania	May 16, 1986	12	*		
	June 15, 1987	14	*		
	June 19, 1989	12		*	
Mozambique	June 16, 1987	19	*		
	June 14, 1990	30		*	
Niger	Nov. 20, 1986	12	*		
	Apr. 21, 1988	13	*		
	Dec. 16, 1988	12		*	
	Sep. 18, 1990	28		*	
Senegal	Nov. 21, 1986	16	*		
	Nov. 17, 1987	12	*		
	Jan. 24, 1989	14		*	
	Feb. 12, 1990	12		*	
	June 21, 1991	12		*	
Tanzania	Sep. 18, 1986	12	*		
	Dec. 13, 1988	6		*	
	Mar. 16, 1990	12		*	
	Jan. 21, 1992	30			*
Togo	Mar. 22, 1988	15	*		
	June 20, 1989	14		*	
	July 9, 1990	24		*	
	June 19, 1992	12			*
Uganda	June 19, 1987	12	*		
	Jan. 26, 1989	18		*	
	June 17, 1992	17			*

Table A9. Central Government Fiscal Profiles Over SAF/ESAF Period

(In percent of GDP)

	1983	1984	1985	1986	1987	1988	1989	1990	1991
Bangladesh[1]				**SAF**				**ESAF**	
Revenue	8.2	8.9	9.1	8.9	9.0	9.1	9.2	9.5	11.0
Current	8.2	8.9	9.1	8.9	9.0	9.1	9.2	9.5	11.0
Tax	6.8	7.1	7.1	7.2	7.2	7.4	7.6	7.6	8.8
Grants	...	...	...	...	...	...	...	...	...
Expenditure	17.3	16.3	16.6	17.3	16.1	16.4	16.8	16.3	16.3
Current	7.7	7.6	7.5	7.7	8.1	8.6	8.6	8.6	8.8
Noninterest	6.9	6.8	6.6	6.9	7.3	7.6	7.7	7.3	7.5
Interest	0.8	0.8	0.9	0.8	0.8	1.0	0.9	1.3	1.3
Capital	9.6	8.7	9.1	9.6	8.0	7.8	8.2	7.7	7.5
Primary current account	1.3	2.1	2.5	2.0	1.7	1.5	1.5	2.2	3.5
Current account	0.5	1.3	1.6	1.2	0.9	0.5	0.6	0.9	2.2
Overall balance	...	...	...	...	...	...	...	...	...
Overall balance (ex grants)	−9.1	−7.4	−7.5	−8.4	−7.1	−7.3	−7.6	−6.8	−5.3
Bolivia					**SAF**	**ESAF**			
Revenue		3.1	9.7	16.3	14.9	15.2	15.3	16.6	17.4
Current		3.1	9.7	16.2	14.7	15.1	15.3	16.5	17.3
Tax		2.9	2.8	4.4	6.8	8.1	8.3	9.0	9.2
Grants		—	—	1.1	0.3	0.5	0.7	1.3	1.3
Expenditure		23.7	21.4	18.7	19.2	20.8	20.4	20.2	20.6
Current		22.3	19.5	17.2	17.8	18.1	16.9	17.4	18.0
Noninterest		20.1	13.7	12.1	13.9	14.3	13.6	14.6	15.2
Interest		2.2	5.8	5.1	3.9	3.8	3.3	2.8	2.8
Capital		1.4	1.9	1.5	1.4	2.7	3.5	2.8	2.6
Primary current account		−17.0	−4.0	4.1	0.8	0.8	1.7	2.0	2.1
Current account		−19.2	−9.8	−1.0	−3.1	−3.0	−1.6	−0.9	−0.7
Overall balance		−20.5	−11.7	−1.3	−4.0	−5.1	−4.4	−2.2	−1.8
Overall balance (ex grants)		−20.5	−11.7	−2.4	−4.3	−5.6	−5.1	−3.5	−3.1
Burundi				**SAF**					**ESAF**
Revenue	12.5	14.1	13.2	16.0	13.6	15.0	18.2	15.7	16.8
Current	12.5	14.1	13.2	16.0	13.6	15.0	18.2	15.7	16.8
Tax	11.5	13.3	12.6	14.4	12.3	13.7	14.8	13.2	14.8
Grants	3.6	4.0	3.5	3.5	4.0	2.4	7.0	8.3	8.3
Expenditure	31.3	27.3	23.4	24.5	30.3	26.6	27.8	29.1	29.1
Current	13.4	10.7	10.7	12.7	13.3	14.9	15.0	15.7	13.2
Noninterest	12.6	9.4	8.8	10.7	11.3	12.8	12.8	13.9	11.7
Interest	0.8	1.3	1.9	2.0	2.0	2.0	2.2	1.8	1.5
Capital	17.9	16.6	12.7	11.8	17.0	11.7	12.8	13.4	15.9
Primary current account	−0.1	4.7	4.3	5.3	2.3	2.2	5.4	1.8	5.1
Current account	−0.9	3.4	2.5	3.3	0.3	0.1	3.2	0.0	3.6
Overall balance	−15.2	−9.2	−6.8	−5.0	−12.8	−9.2	−2.7	−5.1	−4.0
Overall balance (ex grants)	−18.8	−13.2	−10.2	−8.5	−16.7	−11.6	−9.6	−13.4	−12.4
Gambia, The[1]				**SAF**		**ESAF**			
Revenue	20.7	19.0	19.6	22.1	20.4	23.2	21.7	19.8	20.9
Current	20.7	19.0	19.3	22.1	20.2	22.9	21.4	19.3	20.7
Tax	...	17.5	17.6	20.6	18.5	21.1	19.5	19.4	19.0
Grants	4.3	4.1	5.4	10.5	9.6	5.9	6.4	5.4	5.0
Expenditure	34.1	33.5	26.5	36.8	36.8	26.0	29.9	24.0	25.0
Current	22.8	19.4	17.1	22.0	26.9	18.3	18.5	16.8	15.7
Noninterest	20.0	15.6	13.6	16.9	22.8	13.9	14.4	12.9	12.3
Interest	2.8	3.7	3.5	5.1	4.1	4.4	4.1	3.9	3.4
Capital	11.4	14.2	9.4	14.8	9.9	7.7	11.4	7.2	9.3
Primary current account	0.7	3.3	5.7	5.2	−2.6	9.1	7.0	6.4	8.4
Current account	−2.1	−0.5	2.2	0.1	−6.7	4.7	2.9	2.5	5.0
Overall balance	−9.3	−10.4	−1.5	−4.2	−6.8	3.1	−1.8	1.2	0.9
Overall balance (ex grants)	−13.5	−14.6	−6.9	−14.7	−16.4	−2.8	−8.2	−4.2	−4.1

Table A9 (continued)
(In percent of GDP)

	1983	1984	1985	1986	1987	1988	1989	1990	1991
Ghana					**SAF**	**ESAF**			
Revenue	5.5	8.0	11.2	13.7	14.1	13.5	13.6	12.5	15.0
Current	5.5	8.0	11.2	13.7	14.1	13.5	13.6	12.5	15.0
Tax	4.6	6.6	9.4	12.2	12.7	12.3	12.3	11.5	13.5
Grants	0.1	0.8	1.2	2.2	2.6	2.6	3.2	3.2	3.2
Expenditure	8.2	11.1	15.4	19.2	19.1	18.9	18.9	18.1	19.8
Current	7.4	8.6	11.2	11.9	11.2	10.9	11.2	10.8	11.6
Noninterest	5.6	7.3	9.7	9.7	9.8	9.8	9.9	9.4	9.8
Interest	1.8	1.3	1.5	2.2	1.4	1.1	1.3	1.4	1.8
Capital	0.8	2.5	4.2	7.3	7.9	8.0	7.7	7.3	8.2
Primary current account	−0.1	0.7	1.5	4.0	4.3	3.7	3.7	3.1	5.2
Current account	−1.9	−0.6	—	1.8	2.9	2.6	2.4	1.7	3.4
Overall balance	−2.7	−1.8	−2.2	0.1	0.5	0.4	0.7	0.2	1.6
Overall balance (ex grants)	−2.7	−2.1	−2.7	−0.7	−0.3	−0.7	−0.8	−1.3	0.1
Guinea					**SAF**				**ESAF**
Revenue				13.1	14.9	14.0	11.4	12.7	11.9
Current				13.1	14.9	14.0	11.4	12.7	11.9
Tax				1.5	2.2	3.2	3.7	4.2	5.4
Grants				1.9	3.8	3.2	3.3	3.5	3.5
Expenditure				20.5	22.6	23.7	20.3	22.1	19.9
Current				13.0	13.2	13.1	10.7	10.7	10.5
Noninterest				10.4	10.6	10.1	8.5	8.2	8.6
Interest				2.6	2.5	3.1	2.2	2.5	1.9
Capital				7.5	9.4	10.6	9.6	11.4	9.4
Primary current account				2.7	4.3	3.9	2.9	4.5	3.3
Current account				0.1	1.8	0.8	0.7	2.0	1.4
Overall balance				−5.5	−3.8	−6.6	−5.5	−5.8	−4.4
Overall balance (ex grants)				−7.4	−7.6	−9.7	−8.8	−9.4	−8.0
Guyana								**ESAF**	
Revenue				43.8	32.8	39.7	38.7	40.7	40.2
Current				43.7	32.8	39.7	38.7	40.7	40.2
Tax				39.6	29.6	36.5	34.4	38.4	36.7
Grants				1.1	2.9	1.4	2.8	4.7	1.2
Expenditure				96.4	85.5	78.0	90.0	94.3	74.5
Current				81.3	68.9	66.7	76.4	75.6	64.1
Noninterest				38.8	34.2	35.3	33.5	29.6	25.9
Interest				42.5	34.7	31.4	42.9	46.0	38.2
Capital				15.0	16.6	11.3	13.6	18.7	10.4
Primary current account				4.9	−1.4	4.4	5.2	11.1	14.3
Current account				−37.6	−36.1	−27.0	−37.7	−34.9	−23.9
Overall balance				−51.5	−49.8	−36.7	−48.4	−48.9	−33.2
Overall balance (ex grants)				−52.6	−52.7	−38.1	−51.2	−53.6	−34.3
Kenya[1]						**SAF**	**ESAF**		
Revenues			22.3	22.5	23.2	23.1	23.0	22.1	22.4
Current			22.3	22.5	23.2	23.1	23.0	22.1	22.4
Tax			19.5	20.0	20.7	19.8	19.3	19.2	19.5
Grants			1.0	1.0	2.3	2.3	2.9	1.9	2.1
Expenditure			29.3	30.2	28.4	30.2	30.6	30.5	27.8
Current			23.6	22.2	21.9	23.1	22.5	23.1	21.0
Noninterest			18.7	17.5	16.6	17.2	16.9	16.9	15.9
Interest			4.9	4.7	5.3	5.9	5.6	6.2	5.1
Capital			5.7	8.0	6.5	7.1	8.1	7.4	6.8
Primary current account			3.6	5.0	6.6	5.9	6.1	5.2	6.5
Current account			−1.3	0.3	1.3	0.0	0.5	−1.0	1.4
Overall balance			−6.0	−6.6	−2.9	−4.8	−4.8	−6.4	−3.3
Overall balance (ex grants)			−7.0	−7.6	−5.2	−7.1	−7.6	−8.4	−5.4

Table A9 (continued)
(In percent of GDP)

	1983	1984	1985	1986	1987	1988	1989	1990	1991
Lesotho[1] (in percent of GDP)						**SAF**			**ESAF**
Revenue			22.7	21.5	19.2	18.9	22.7	23.0	25.3
Current			22.7	21.5	19.2	18.9	22.7	23.0	25.3
Tax			20.0	18.7	16.7	16.7	19.2	20.2	21.9
Grants			0.9	2.1	4.0	5.0	6.6	6.9	4.8
Expenditure			29.8	30.5	33.5	33.2	33.7	31.4	30.7
Current			20.5	21.6	19.4	19.7	18.8	16.7	19.7
Noninterest			18.6	19.4	17.5	17.5	14.6	13.5	17.0
Interest			1.9	2.2	1.9	2.2	4.2	3.2	2.7
Capital			9.3	8.9	14.1	13.5	14.9	14.7	11.0
Primary current account			4.1	2.1	1.7	1.4	8.1	9.5	8.3
Current account			2.2	−0.1	−0.2	−0.8	3.9	6.3	5.6
Overall balance			−6.2	−6.9	−10.3	−9.3	−4.4	−0.6	−0.6
Overall balance (ex grants)			−7.1	−9.0	−14.3	−14.3	−11.0	−7.5	−5.4
Madagascar					**SAF**		**ESAF**		
Revenue		16.9	12.9	12.1	14.7	13.1	11.3	11.7	8.6
Current		16.9	12.9	12.1	14.7	13.1	11.3	11.7	8.6
Tax		11.7	10.0	9.3	11.0	10.5	8.8	9.4	6.9
Grants		0.9	0.4	0.7	0.7	0.7	4.1	4.4	2.1
Expenditure		21.8	17.2	16.2	18.7	17.1	20.7	17.0	16.6
Current		13.9	11.2	10.8	11.7	10.2	11.0	9.1	9.9
Noninterest		13.9	9.7	9.2	9.6	8.1	8.3	7.6	7.9
Interest		0.0	1.5	1.6	2.1	2.1	2.7	1.5	2.0
Capital		7.9	6.0	5.4	7.0	6.9	9.7	7.9	6.7
Primary current account		3.0	3.2	2.9	5.1	5.0	3.0	4.1	0.7
Current account		3.0	1.7	1.3	3.0	2.9	0.3	2.6	−1.3
Overall balance		−4.0	−3.9	−3.5	−3.4	−3.3	−5.1	−0.8	−5.6
Overall balance (ex grants)		−4.9	−4.3	−4.2	−4.1	−4.0	−9.2	−5.2	−7.7
Malawi[1]						**ESAF**			
Revenue			22.0	21.1	20.7	21.3	21.8	19.6	18.4
Current			22.0	21.1	20.7	21.3	21.8	19.6	18.4
Tax			17.9	16.8	16.0	17.9	18.5	16.6	16.3
Grants			2.2	3.4	2.7	5.7	4.6	2.1	3.3
Expenditure			32.0	34.2	30.4	28.7	29.5	25.7	23.8
Current			22.8	24.0	22.7	19.9	21.6	19.9	17.4
Noninterest			16.8	17.5	16.5	15.5	16.3	16.6	14.7
Interest			6.0	6.5	6.2	4.4	5.3	3.3	2.7
Capital			9.2	10.2	7.7	8.8	7.9	5.8	6.4
Primary current account			5.2	3.6	4.2	5.8	5.5	3.0	3.7
Current account			−0.8	−2.9	−2.0	1.4	0.2	−0.3	1.0
Overall balance			−7.8	−9.6	−7.0	−1.6	−2.0	−4.6	−3.0
Overall balance (ex grants)			−10.0	−13.0	−9.7	−7.3	−6.6	−6.7	−6.3
Mauritania					**SAF**		**ESAF**		
Revenue		24.3	23.7	23.9	25.6	24.7	23.1	24.6	22.3
Current		24.3	23.7	23.9	25.6	24.7	23.1	24.6	22.3
Tax		18.5	19.7	19.0	18.1	18.4	17.5	18.3	16.6
Grants		6.7	4.6	2.3	4.8	1.6	2.6	2.1	1.7
Expenditure		42.1	33.1	28.9	36.7	36.1	41.3	36.8	29.4
Current		24.7	22.4	21.4	21.6	21.1	20.5	21.4	22.0
Noninterest		22.5	19.6	17.8	18.5	18.2	17.2	18.9	19.4
Interest		2.2	2.8	3.6	3.1	3.0	3.2	2.6	2.6
Capital		17.4	10.7	7.5	15.2	15.0	20.8	15.4	7.4
Primary current account		1.8	4.1	6.1	7.1	6.6	5.9	5.7	2.9
Current account		−0.4	1.3	2.4	4.0	3.6	2.6	3.1	0.3
Overall balance		−10.7	−4.5	−2.4	−3.3	−6.1	−8.0	−5.7	−4.1
Overall balance (ex grants)		−17.5	−9.1	−4.8	−8.1	−7.7	−10.6	−7.8	−5.8

Table A9 (continued)
(In percent of GDP)

	1983	1984	1985	1986	1987	1988	1989	1990	1991
Mozambique					**SAF**			**ESAF**	
Revenue		20.7	13.1	13.3	16.0	19.9	23.4	22.3	23.5
Current		20.7	13.1	13.3	16.0	19.9	23.4	22.3	23.5
Tax		15.0	9.1	9.4	13.6	16.7	20.7	19.9	19.9
Grants		2.7	2.0	2.3	9.3	14.0	16.5	16.9	20.8
Expenditure		41.5	27.0	30.9	37.5	45.2	48.9	51.5	50.3
Current		26.0	22.4	25.4	21.3	22.6	25.5	25.6	24.0
Noninterest		25.9	22.3	24.9	19.3	20.3	22.3	22.2	21.6
Interest		0.1	0.1	0.5	2.0	2.3	3.2	3.4	2.4
Capital		15.5	4.6	5.5	16.2	22.6	23.4	25.9	26.3
Primary current account		−5.2	−9.2	−11.6	−3.3	−0.4	1.1	0.1	1.9
Current account		−5.3	−9.3	−12.1	−5.3	−2.7	−2.1	−3.3	−0.5
Overall balance		−18.1	−11.9	−15.3	−11.9	−11.4	−8.9	−12.4	−6.0
Overall balance (ex grants)		−20.8	−13.9	−17.7	−21.5	−25.3	−25.4	−29.3	−26.8
Niger[1]					**SAF**		**ESAF**		
Revenue		11.1	11.2	11.3	10.1	10.1	10.4	10.2	8.6
Current		11.1	11.2	11.3	10.1	10.1	10.4	10.2	8.6
Tax		9.5	9.4	8.6	8.0	8.0	8.2	7.8	7.2
Grants		3.7	4.9	5.2	4.7	4.7	4.8	5.4	3.9
Expenditure		19.6	20.9	20.1	19.4	20.5	20.9	22.3	15.8
Current		11.1	11.4	11.3	11.5	11.6	11.8	13.0	11.1
Noninterest		8.4	8.4	8.5	8.7	9.0	9.2	10.9	9.3
Interest		2.7	3.0	2.8	2.8	2.6	2.6	2.1	1.8
Capital		8.5	9.5	8.8	7.9	8.9	9.1	9.3	4.7
Primary current account		2.7	2.8	2.8	1.4	1.1	1.2	−0.7	−0.7
Current account		0.0	−0.2	0.0	−1.4	−1.5	−1.4	−2.8	−2.5
Overall balance		−4.8	−4.8	−3.6	−4.6	−5.7	−5.7	−6.7	−3.3
Overall balance (ex grants)		−8.5	−9.7	−8.8	−9.3	−10.4	−10.5	−12.1	−7.2
Senegal[1]				**SAF**		**ESAF**			
Revenue	19.4	18.8	17.6	18.8	17.5	16.9	17.0	19.0	18.6
Current	19.4	18.8	17.6	18.8	17.5	16.9	17.0	19.0	18.6
Tax	18.1	17.5	14.9	14.6	14.3	13.5	14.3	15.2	15.9
Grants	1.2	1.1	1.6	1.1	1.4	2.0	1.3	1.7	1.2
Expenditure	25.2	23.5	21.4	21.4	20.1	21.0	21.3	18.7	19.6
Current	21.0	20.0	17.7	17.4	17.1	17.1	16.6	14.6	14.1
Noninterest	17.2	15.9	14.4	14.4	13.9	13.8	13.9	12.2	11.9
Interest	3.8	4.1	3.3	3.0	3.2	3.3	2.7	2.4	2.2
Capital	4.2	3.5	3.7	4.0	3.0	3.9	4.7	4.1	5.5
Primary current account	2.2	2.9	3.2	4.4	3.6	3.1	3.1	6.8	6.7
Current account	−1.6	−1.2	−0.1	1.4	−0.4	−0.2	0.4	4.4	4.5
Overall balance	−4.6	−3.6	−2.3	−1.5	−1.2	−2.1	−3.0	1.9	0.2
Overall balance (ex grants)	−5.8	−4.7	−3.9	−2.6	−2.6	−4.1	−4.3	0.2	−1.0
Sri Lanka						**SAF**			**ESAF**
Revenue			22.3	20.7	21.4	18.8	21.4	21.1	20.3
Current			22.3	20.7	21.4	18.8	21.4	21.1	20.3
Tax			18.7	17.4	17.9	16.2	18.9	19.0	18.2
Grants			2.0	2.1	2.4	3.0	2.5	2.1	2.1
Expenditure			34.0	33.0	32.5	34.5	32.6	31.0	31.8
Current			21.6	18.9	20.1	20.8	22.6	22.3	22.3
Noninterest			17.0	14.0	14.9	15.1	16.9	15.9	16.4
Interest			4.6	4.9	5.2	5.7	5.7	6.4	5.9
Capital			12.4	14.1	12.4	13.7	10.0	8.7	9.5
Primary current account			5.3	6.7	6.5	3.7	4.5	5.2	3.9
Current account			0.7	1.8	1.3	−2.0	−1.2	−1.2	−2.0
Overall balance			−9.7	−10.2	−8.7	−12.7	−8.7	−7.8	−9.4
Overall balance (ex grants)			−11.7	−12.3	−11.1	−15.7	−11.2	−9.9	−11.5

Table A9 (concluded)

(In percent of GDP)

	1983	1984	1985	1986	1987	1988	1989	1990	1991
Tanzania[1]					**SAF**				**ESAF**
Revenue		17.1	14.9	16.1	16.7	19.5	21.0	22.1	23.5
Current		17.1	14.9	16.1	16.7	19.5	21.0	22.1	23.5
Tax		16.3	14.0	15.1	15.3	17.1	18.1	19.6	20.7
Grants		0.0	—	5.9	5.7	5.7	6.1	3.8	4.4
Expenditure		24.3	23.1	24.6	26.3	25.5	28.0	25.2	26.4
Current		18.8	19.2	18.2	18.6	21.2	23.0	22.5	21.9
Noninterest		16.4	17.2	14.8	14.8	17.2	19.3	19.2	18.7
Interest		2.4	2.0	3.4	3.8	4.0	3.7	3.3	3.2
Capital		5.5	3.9	6.4	7.7	4.3	5.0	2.7	4.5
Primary current account		0.7	−2.3	1.3	1.9	2.3	1.7	2.9	4.8
Current account		−1.7	−4.3	−2.1	−1.9	−1.7	−2.0	−0.4	1.6
Overall balance		−7.2	−8.2	−2.6	−3.9	−0.3	−0.9	0.7	1.5
Overall balance (ex grants)		−7.2	−8.2	−8.5	−9.6	−6.0	−7.0	−3.1	−2.9
Togo						**SAF**	**ESAF**		
Revenue			29.9	28.5	23.7	23.4	22.6	22.5	17.1
Current			29.9	28.5	23.7	23.4	22.6	22.5	17.1
Tax			22.9	21.4	19.6	19.4	19.5	18.5	15.0
Grants			4.7	4.2	2.2	2.0	2.4	3.2	1.5
Expenditure			36.1	37.2	32.8	28.7	28.8	28.6	24.5
Current			23.5	22.6	23.1	21.5	21.3	21.3	20.1
Noninterest			16.8	17.7	19.0	17.3	17.1	18.0	16.9
Interest			6.6	4.9	4.1	4.2	4.2	3.2	3.1
Capital			12.7	14.6	9.7	7.2	7.5	7.3	4.4
Primary current account			13.1	10.8	4.7	6.1	5.5	4.5	0.2
Current account			6.4	5.9	0.6	1.9	1.3	1.2	−3.0
Overall balance			−1.6	−4.5	−6.9	−3.3	−3.8	−2.9	−5.9
Overall balance (ex grants)			−6.3	−8.7	−9.1	−5.3	−6.2	−6.1	−7.4
Uganda[1]					**SAF**		**ESAF**		
Revenue		4.9	7.0	4.9	6.6	6.3	7.6	8.1	7.0
Current		4.9	7.0	4.9	6.6	6.3	7.6	8.1	7.0
Tax		4.9	7.0	4.1	5.8	5.3	6.9	7.6	6.7
Grants		0.2	1.3	0.5	1.9	1.8	1.6	4.2	7.3
Expenditure		14.4	12.2	9.4	13.0	12.0	14.0	16.3	21.8
Current		10.7	9.1	5.8	7.2	8.0	7.9	8.1	12.1
Noninterest		9.9	7.7	5.4	6.6	7.2	7.2	6.6	8.7
Interest		0.8	1.5	0.4	0.7	0.8	0.7	1.5	3.4
Capital		3.7	3.1	3.6	5.8	4.0	6.1	8.2	9.7
Primary current account		−5.0	−0.7	−0.5	0.0	−0.9	0.4	1.5	−1.7
Current account		−5.8	−2.1	−0.9	−0.6	−1.7	−0.3	0.0	−5.1
Overall balance		−9.2	−3.9	−4.0	−4.5	−3.9	−4.8	−4.0	−7.5
Overall balance (ex grants)		−9.5	−5.2	−4.5	−6.4	−5.7	−6.4	−8.2	−14.8

Source: IMF staff estimates.

Note: Except for Guinea, data are shown for the period commencing three full fiscal years before the first SAF- or ESAF-supported program.

[1] Fiscal year. For Niger, calendar year for 1989–91.

Table A10. Exchange Rate Developments Against Major Currencies (SDR Exchange Rates)[1]
(1980 = 100)

	1985	1986	1987	1988	1989	1990	1991
I. Countries with depreciating currencies during their SAF/ESAF arrangements							
Bangladesh		**SAF**				**ESAF**	
Nominal	71.1	56.3	50.2	47.1	48.5	42.9	40.1
Real	95.7	82.8	79.2	79.4	86.6	78.8	76.1
Bolivia		**SAF**	**ESAF**				
Nominal	66.8	1.4	1.2	1.0	0.9	0.7	0.7
Real	241.4	73.2	69.9	66.4	67.2	60.2	61.8
Burundi		**SAF**					**ESAF**
Nominal	95.6	87.9	73.3	62.5	57.7	50.4	47.5
Real	112.2	103.2	90.4	78.7	77.8	69.5	69.1
Gambia, The		**SAF**		**ESAF**			
Nominal	57.0	28.1	24.5	24.9	23.1	21.0	18.7
Real	82.7	61.4	66.1	73.1	70.7	68.6	63.9
Ghana			**SAF**	**ESAF**			
Nominal	6.5	3.4	1.9	1.3	1.0	0.8	0.7
Real	45.7	29.4	21.8	19.9	18.8	19.2	19.2
Guinea			**SAF**				**ESAF**
Nominal	...	6.2	4.5	3.9	3.3	2.8	2.4
Real	...	...	...	...	...	...	...
Guyana						**ESAF**	
Nominal	77.0	66.3	26.6	24.7	12.3	6.4	2.4
Real	145.1	132.4	66.6	85.1	69.0	60.3	42.3
Kenya				**SAF**	**ESAF**		
Nominal	58.2	50.9	45.6	40.7	36.9	31.2	25.8
Real	83.8	75.1	69.2	65.3	62.4	56.2	51.3
Lesotho				**SAF**			**ESAF**
Nominal	45.8	38.1	38.5	33.3	30.2	28.9	26.8
Real	66.4	63.9	70.9	66.7	66.7	68.0	71.5
Madagascar			**SAF**		**ESAF**		
Nominal	40.9	35.0	21.4	14.6	13.4	13.6	11.0
Real	78.6	75.6	51.0	44.1	42.3	45.7	38.9
Malawi				**ESAF**			
Nominal	61.1	48.6	37.1	30.8	29.9	28.6	27.6
Real	82.7	74.2	71.2	75.3	80.5	82.0	85.0
Mauritania				**SAF**	**ESAF**		
Nominal	76.4	68.5	62.5	59.1	55.2	54.4	52.9
Real	96.9	92.2	89.2	83.6	84.4	83.7	82.2
Mozambique			**SAF**			**ESAF**	
Nominal	96.2	88.9	17.8	6.1	4.5	3.4	2.2
Real	...	...	...	...	...	...	...
Sri Lanka				**SAF**			**ESAF**
Nominal	78.0	65.4	56.5	50.3	46.7	39.5	38.0
Real	106.2	93.1	82.4	81.9	78.9	77.9	80.8
Tanzania			**SAF**				**ESAF**
Nominal	60.2	34.4	13.1	8.1	5.9	4.0	3.6
Real	169.4	121.7	60.6	48.2	42.5	33.5	36.0
Uganda			**SAF**		**ESAF**		
Nominal	1.51	0.59	0.27	0.08	0.04	0.02	0.01
Real	14.5	15.2	19.6	17.9	15.3	9.6	7.2
II. Countries with appreciating currencies during their SAF/ESAF arrangements							
Niger			**SAF**		**ESAF**		
Nominal	60.6	67.7	70.7	68.7	67.3	74.5	71.4
Real	67.1	71.4	68.3	63.9	58.2	61.0	52.3
Senegal		**SAF**		**ESAF**			
Nominal	60.6	67.7	70.7	68.7	67.3	74.5	71.4
Real	81.9	95.6	93.8	87.4	82.4	87.4	78.2
Togo				**SAF**	**ESAF**		
Nominal	60.6	67.7	70.7	68.7	67.3	74.5	71.4
Real	64.4	73.7	75.5	71.5	66.6	71.0	65.9

Source: IMF staff calculations.

[1]SDR per unit of domestic currency. Real exchange rates are computed in relation to an SDR inflation rate calculated as a weighted average of the consumer price index (CPI) inflation rates of France, Germany, Japan, the United Kingdom, and the United States.

Table A11. Exchange Rate Developments: Effective Exchange Rate Indices
(1980 = 100)

	1985	1986	1987	1988	1989	1990	1991
I. Countries with depreciating currencies in nominal effective terms during their SAF/ESAF arrangements							
Bangladesh		**SAF**				**ESAF**	
Nominal effective	89.9	73.6	68.3	66.3	72.1	72.9	72.6
Real effective	107.7	93.6	90.2	87.8	93.7	88.5	86.7
Burundi		**SAF**					**ESAF**
Nominal effective	130.2	114.0	94.6	83.1	79.4	68.3	66.8
Real effective	135.3	116.4	99.7	87.7	88.8	77.1	77.3
Gambia, The		**SAF**		**ESAF**			
Nominal effective	91.5	45.7	41.3	45.0	47.2	49.3	48.2
Real effective	99.3	71.4	75.3	81.5	78.4	73.5	69.6
Ghana			**SAF**	**ESAF**			
Nominal effective	9.8	4.9	2.9	2.4	2.2	1.9	1.9
Real effective	53.2	30.6	23.6	22.5	21.2	21.1	21.9
Guyana						**ESAF**	
Nominal effective	105.7	100.1	43.9	44.7	24.5	12.6	6.0
Real effective	153.5	145.6	75.0	94.1	74.5	52.7	45.4
Kenya				**SAF**	**ESAF**		
Nominal effective	86.6	77.1	71.6	68.4	68.2	64.4	58.4
Real effective	101.3	88.6	82.0	77.9	76.6	70.5	69.0
Madagascar			**SAF**		**ESAF**		
Nominal effective	66.0	58.8	38.6	29.5	30.0	34.0	30.6
Real effective	92.7	87.6	59.7	52.0	49.6	52.4	45.7
Mozambique			**SAF**			**ESAF**	
Nominal effective	154.6	146.6	29.0	10.5	8.0	6.0	4.1
Real effective	248.7	305.7	124.8	79.0	79.1	78.8	65.6
Sri Lanka				**SAF**			**ESAF**
Nominal effective	88.2	75.6	66.7	59.5	55.2	48.4	47.8
Real effective	116.8	103.9	93.0	90.9	86.1	87.7	92.3
Tanzania			**SAF**				**ESAF**
Nominal effective	207.9	143.9	70.8	55.5	48.5	37.2	39.8
Real effective	92.3	53.4	21.3	14.3	11.6	9.2	9.1
Uganda			**SAF**		**ESAF**		
Nominal effective	3.0	1.3	0.7	0.2	0.1	0.1	0.1
Real effective	17.5	18.4	23.6	21.3	18.1	11.0	8.4
II. Countries with appreciating currencies in nominal effective terms during their SAF/ESAF arrangements							
Bolivia		**SAF**	**ESAF**				
Nominal effective	0.29	0.01	0.01	0.01	0.03	0.06	0.09
Real effective	296.7	87.5	84.3	80.0	76.8	64.8	66.9
Malawi				**ESAF**			
Nominal effective	94.4	80.8	64.2	58.4	62.7	67.8	73.3
Real effective	97.8	87.9	81.7	86.5	91.7	92.0	97.5
Mauritania				**SAF**	**ESAF**		
Nominal effective	126.6	116.8	112.5	119.4	128.2	154.1	171.9
Real effective	112.0	101.9	96.4	89.0	87.9	84.6	85.8
Senegal		**SAF**		**ESAF**			
Nominal effective	99.0	105.7	109.8	111.7	116.8	129.3	130.6
Real effective	103.2	112.1	106.3	100.0	95.5	94.8	88.2
Togo				**SAF**	**ESAF**		
Nominal effective	95.6	104.7	110.5	113.8	119.6	140.8	146.0
Real effective	81.4	87.7	87.2	82.1	76.5	78.7	75.2
III. Countries with stable currencies in nominal effective terms during their SAF/ESAF arrangements							
Lesotho				**SAF**			**ESAF**
Nominal effective	97.5	96.4	96.4	95.8	95.5	95.2	95.1
Real effective	96.3	94.8	91.8	90.7	90.8	88.7	90.5
Niger			**SAF**		**ESAF**		
Nominal effective	88.3	88.4	88.5	86.9	86.3	89.4	88.0
Real effective	83.9	79.0	71.8	67.7	62.8	62.1	54.2

Source: IMF staff estimates.

Table A12. Export Values Relative to Domestic Consumer Price Indices[1]
(1990 = 100)

	1985	1986	1987	1988	1989	1990	1991
Bangladesh	131	118	109	105	101	100	99
Bolivia	332	212	156	122	99	100	117
Burundi	206	115	117	71	78	100	102
Gambia, The	199	142	128	111	103	100	96
Ghana	2,079	403	150	98	91	100	109
Guinea	...	...	120	111	99	100	109
Guyana	...	...	585	206	97	100	73
Kenya	297	170	150	109	98	100	95
Lesotho	...	135	102	96	94	100	104
Madagascar	370	139	78	75	81	100	94
Malawi	209	136	99	96	92	100	97
Mauritania	140	113	110	96	93	100	98
Mozambique	37,234	1,879	212	103	86	100	84
Niger	84	82	78	82	86	100	105
Senegal	106	117	118	108	102	100	99
Sri Lanka	186	183	128	107	98	100	105
Tanzania	...	916	276	139	104	100	101
Togo	68	84	95	99	94	100	100
Uganda	90,914	6,899	843	191	91	100	106

Source: IMF staff estimates.
[1]Calculated as the ratio of export unit values to the consumer price index.

Table A13. Sustainability: Evolution of the External Debt to Export Ratio During SAF/ESAF Period[1]

	External Debt to Export Ratio (In percent)			Change in Debt to Export Ratio (Percent change)	Change in External Debt (Percent change)	Analysis of Change in External Debt to Export Ratio								Memorandum Items		
	Prior to first SAF or ESAF[2]	Prior to first ESAF[2]	Most recent year[2]			Non-interest current account deficit[3]	Non-debt-creating flows[3]	Increase in gross reserves[3]	Debt reduction[4]	Real interest less export growth[5] (In percent)	Terms of trade loss[6] (In percent)	Cross-product and exchange rate[7] (In percent)	Residual discrepancy[8] (In percent)	Real interest rate[9] (In percent)	Export volume growth rate (In percent)	Number of years
I. Countries with significant decline in debt to export ratio[10]																
Gambia, The	381	318	207	−45.7	−4.6	64.8	−112.0	30.3	−8.5	−47.7	5.1	20.5	3.6	0.1	6.8	6
Guyana	903	903	775	−14.2	0.1	3.6	−5.8	3.2	−13.2	−10.8	5.4	5.2	−1.9	−1.8	3.5	2
Togo	212	182	166	−21.5	−2.9	42.0	−48.0	7.9	−13.3	−9.3	3.4	−2.2	−2.6	1.8	4.0	4
Bolivia	523	665	422	−19.3	5.2	34.5	−31.4	—	−44.3	−39.7	24.7	27.5	13.1	1.1	7.8	5
Senegal	271	316	215	−20.7	−12.0	54.7	−36.0	7.6	−25.4	25.4	−8.2	−17.0	−21.6	4.7	1.0	6
Malawi	345	345	297	−14.0	40.2	81.1	−70.1	1.5	−3.1	−25.3	−12.7	5.5	11.9	1.7	7.2	4
Bangladesh	493	448	406	−17.7	70.2	80.8	−44.4	16.3	—	−73.9	−3.7	17.0	−10.6	0.1	9.7	6
Mozambique	1,816	2,083	1,566	−13.8	78.8	102.9	−74.5	7.5	−18.0	−77.8	9.1	21.6	21.9	0.2	12.3	5
II. Countries with broadly unchanged debt to export ratio[10]																
Sri Lanka	225	201	216	−4.1	29.8	39.5	−29.9	9.8	—	−19.1	4.6	−0.2	−8.4	1.3	5.6	4
Kenya	239	236	231	−3.4	10.2	38.2	−31.2	−2.0	−15.3	1.1	6.0	0.6	−0.9	2.0	1.8	4
Guinea	305	254	293	−4.2	25.3	55.8	−28.4	5.4	−13.3	−28.9	16.0	−0.4	−9.7	−1.1	4.3	5
Mauritania	328	328	323	−1.4	−8.7	39.9	−35.7	0.4	−17.4	13.5	10.9	−2.8	−9.2	0.7	−2.0	5
Ghana	331	343	338	1.9	38.8	43.3	−42.5	16.0	−14.5	−69.3	36.6	28.2	4.3	−2.0	9.8	5
III. Countries with significant increase in debt to export ratio[10]																
Tanzania	568	547	611	7.6	21.8	71.7	−64.9	8.6	−0.5	−7.3	11.8	17.3	−21.3	−1.1	0.4	5
Madagascar	664	727	732	10.3	5.7	14.8	−18.0	−0.9	−17.2	−18.5	36.6	12.9	0.4	3.3	6.4	5
Lesotho	52	64	65	25.3	51.4	500.8	−482.6	47.3	−1.3	−8.3	—	−7.8	−15.4	2.6	4.5	4
Niger	295	375	395	33.9	−0.9	66.4	−53.2	1.2	−33.4	18.3	31.8	4.8	−1.5	3.5	0.1	5
Burundi	352	993	819	132.9	115.8	231.8	−163.4	27.1	−27.8	−24.6	39.6	43.6	2.9	−1.6	2.4	6
Uganda	273	434	1,092	300.8	101.2	115.4	−61.8	2.6	−1.6	8.4	57.4	166.7	3.5	2.7	1.2	5

Source: IMF staff estimates.

[1]Stock of medium- and long-term external public and publicly guaranteed debt (including use of IMF resources) as percent of exports of goods and nonfactor services.

[2]End of calendar year or fiscal year. Most recent year is calendar year 1991 or fiscal year 1991/92.

[3]Percent of initial debt stock; cumulative flows. Noninterest current account excludes grants. Non-debt-creating flows include grants, direct investment, private and short-term capital flows, and errors and omissions. Inflows have negative sign.

[4]Cumulative debt reduction as percent of initial debt stock.

[5]Real interest defined as cumulative interest flow divided by initial debt stock and deflated by import price index.

[6]Cumulative depreciation of terms of trade index (depreciation +).

[7]Cross-currency exchange rate terms and cross-product terms.

[8]Residual discrepancy attributable to mismatch between debt stock and flow data.

[9]Real interest rate (see footnote 5) on annual basis.

[10]Countries listed in order of increasing annual average decline in debt/export ratio (see Table 6).

Table A14. External Current Account Positions

(Excluding official transfers; in percent of GDP)

Country	1985	1986	1987	1988	1989	1990	1991
Bangladesh	−6.9	−5.5	−5.8	−6.9	−6.8	−4.1	−2.9
Bolivia	−8.3	−10.5	−11.8	−11.1	−8.5	−8.3	−9.5
Burundi	−10.5	−11.7	−17.9	−14.6	−14.2	−20.8	−18.1
Gambia, The	−16.5	−21.8	−16.1	−13.1	−18.1	−13.2	−13.9
Ghana	−4.1	−3.5	−4.6	−5.1	−6.0	−8.3	−6.9
Guinea	...	−5.6	−8.2	−12.8	−8.4	−10.3	−10.7
Guyana	...	...	−30.7	−22.4	−41.0	−50.0	−50.0
Kenya	−3.2	−2.5	−8.1	−8.4	−10.5	−7.5	−6.2
Lesotho	−20.1	−14.6	−17.3	−21.5	−23.3	−35.3	−43.5
Madagascar	−10.9	−6.3	−10.0	−10.8	−8.7	−11.8	−10.6
Malawi	−8.5	−5.8	−4.6	−12.5	−19.8	−13.9	−14.3
Mauritania	−26.2	−33.3	−28.6	−22.1	−14.4	−21.7	−14.2
Mozambique	−15.3	−15.3	−47.8	−52.9	−58.8	−54.7	−59.0
Niger	−15.2	−9.8	−9.9	−9.5	−10.4	−11.1	−6.4
Senegal	−13.8	−10.5	−10.8	−9.5	−7.9	−9.0	−7.9
Sri Lanka	−8.9	−15.2	−9.8	−9.9	−9.5	−10.4	−11.1
Tanzania	...	−14.7	−20.1	−26.1	−27.3	−28.0	−27.9
Togo	−12.7	−14.8	−12.7	−11.8	−9.8	−13.3	−10.4
Uganda	...	−6.4	−14.0	−15.4	−16.2	−15.5	−10.9
Average	−12.1	−11.5	−15.2	−15.6	−16.8	−18.3	−17.6

Source: IMF staff estimates.

References

Gotur, Padma, "Bangladesh: Economic Reform Measures and the Poor," IMF Working Paper WP/91/39 (Washington: International Monetary Fund, 1991).

Gulde, Anne-Marie, "Sri Lanka: Price Changes and the Poor," IMF Working Paper WP/91/46 (Washington: International Monetary Fund, 1991).

Hicks, Ronald, and Odd Per Brekk, "Assessing the Impact of Structural Adjustment on the Poor: The Case of Malawi," IMF Working Paper WP/91/112 (Washington: International Monetary Fund, 1991).

Lopes, Paulo S., and Emilio Sacerdoti, "Mozambique: Economic Rehabilitation and the Poor," IMF Working Paper WP/91/101 (Washington: International Monetary Fund, 1991).

World Bank, *Adjustment in Africa: Progress, Payoffs and Challenges,* World Bank Policy Research Report No. 2 (forthcoming).

Recent Occasional Papers of the International Monetary Fund

106. Economic Adjustment in Low-Income Countries: Experience Under the Enhanced Structural Adjustment Facility, by Susan Schadler, Franek Rozwadowski, Siddharth Tiwari, and David O. Robinson. 1993.
105. The Structure and Operation of the World Gold Market, by Gary O'Callaghan. 1993.
104. Price Liberalization in Russia: Behavior of Prices, Household Incomes, and Consumption During the First Year, by Vincent Koen and Steven Phillips. 1993.
103. Liberalization of the Capital Account: Experiences and Issues, by Donald J. Mathieson and Liliana Rojas-Suárez. 1993.
102. Financial Sector Reforms and Exchange Arrangements in Eastern Europe. Part I: Financial Markets and Intermediation, by Guillermo A. Calvo and Manmohan S. Kumar. Part II: Exchange Arrangements of Previously Centrally Planned Economies, by Eduardo Borensztein and Paul R. Masson. 1993.
101. Spain: Converging with the European Community, by Michel Galy, Gonzalo Pastor, and Thierry Pujol. 1993.
100. The Gambia: Economic Adjustment in a Small Open Economy, by Michael T. Hadjimichael, Thomas Rumbaugh, and Eric Verreydt. 1992.
99. Mexico: The Strategy to Achieve Sustained Economic Growth, edited by Claudio Loser and Eliot Kalter. 1992.
98. Albania: From Isolation Toward Reform, by Mario I. Blejer, Mauro Mecagni, Ratna Sahay, Richard Hides, Barry Johnston, Piroska Nagy, and Roy Pepper. 1992.
97. Rules and Discretion in International Economic Policy, by Manuel Guitián. 1992.
96. Policy Issues in the Evolving International Monetary System, by Morris Goldstein, Peter Isard, Paul R. Masson, and Mark P. Taylor. 1992.
95. The Fiscal Dimensions of Adjustment in Low-Income Countries, by Karim Nashashibi, Sanjeev Gupta, Claire Liuksila, Henri Lorie, and Walter Mahler. 1992.
94. Tax Harmonization in the European Community: Policy Issues and Analysis, edited by George Kopits. 1992.
93. Regional Trade Arrangements, by Augusto de la Torre and Margaret R. Kelly. 1992.
92. Stabilization and Structural Reform in the Czech and Slovak Federal Republic: First Stage, by Bijan B. Aghevli, Eduardo Borensztein, and Tessa van der Willigen. 1992.
91. Economic Policies for a New South Africa, edited by Desmond Lachman and Kenneth Bercuson with a staff team comprising Daudi Ballali, Robert Corker, Charalambos Christofides, and James Wein. 1992.
90. The Internationalization of Currencies: An Appraisal of the Japanese Yen, by George S. Tavlas and Yuzuru Ozeki. 1992.
89. The Romanian Economic Reform Program, by Dimitri G. Demekas and Mohsin S. Khan. 1991.
88. Value-Added Tax: Administrative and Policy Issues, edited by Alan A. Tait. 1991.
87. Financial Assistance from Arab Countries and Arab Regional Institutions, by Pierre van den Boogaerde. 1991.
86. Ghana: Adjustment and Growth, 1983–91, by Ishan Kapur, Michael T. Hadjimichael, Paul Hilbers, Jerald Schiff, and Philippe Szymczak. 1991.
85. Thailand: Adjusting to Success—Current Policy Issues, by David Robinson, Yangho Byeon, and Ranjit Teja with Wanda Tseng. 1991.
84. Financial Liberalization, Money Demand, and Monetary Policy in Asian Countries, by Wanda Tseng and Robert Corker. 1991.
83. Economic Reform in Hungary Since 1968, by Anthony R. Boote and Janos Somogyi. 1991.
82. Characteristics of a Successful Exchange Rate System, by Jacob A. Frenkel, Morris Goldstein, and Paul R. Masson. 1991.

81. Currency Convertibility and the Transformation of Centrally Planned Economies, by Joshua E. Greene and Peter Isard. 1991.
80. Domestic Public Debt of Externally Indebted Countries, by Pablo E. Guidotti and Manmohan S. Kumar. 1991.
79. The Mongolian People's Republic: Toward a Market Economy, by Elizabeth Milne, John Leimone, Franek Rozwadowski, and Padej Sukachevin. 1991.
78. Exchange Rate Policy in Developing Countries: Some Analytical Issues, by Bijan B. Aghevli, Mohsin S. Khan, and Peter J. Montiel. 1991.
77. Determinants and Systemic Consequences of International Capital Flows, by Morris Goldstein, Donald J. Mathieson, David Folkerts-Landau, Timothy Lane, J. Saúl Lizondo, and Liliana Rojas-Suárez. 1991.
76. China: Economic Reform and Macroeconomic Management, by Mario Blejer, David Burton, Steven Dunaway, and Gyorgy Szapary. 1991.
75. German Unification: Economic Issues, edited by Leslie Lipschitz and Donogh McDonald. 1990.
74. The Impact of the European Community's Internal Market on the EFTA, by Richard K. Abrams, Peter K. Cornelius, Per L. Hedfors, and Gunnar Tersman. 1990.
73. The European Monetary System: Developments and Perspectives, by Horst Ungerer, Jouko J. Hauvonen, Augusto Lopez-Claros, and Thomas Mayer. 1990.
72. The Czech and Slovak Federal Republic: An Economy in Transition, by Jim Prust and an IMF Staff Team. 1990.
71. MULTIMOD Mark II: A Revised and Extended Model, by Paul Masson, Steven Symansky, and Guy Meredith. 1990.
70. The Conduct of Monetary Policy in the Major Industrial Countries: Instruments and Operating Procedures, by Dallas S. Batten, Michael P. Blackwell, In-Su Kim, Simon E. Nocera, and Yuzuru Ozeki. 1990.
69. International Comparisons of Government Expenditure Revisited: The Developing Countries, 1975–86, by Peter S. Heller and Jack Diamond. 1990.
68. Debt Reduction and Economic Activity, by Michael P. Dooley, David Folkerts-Landau, Richard D. Haas, Steven A. Symansky, and Ralph W. Tryon. 1990.
67. The Role of National Saving in the World Economy: Recent Trends and Prospects, by Bijan B. Aghevli, James M. Boughton, Peter J. Montiel, Delano Villanueva, and Geoffrey Woglom. 1990.
66. The European Monetary System in the Context of the Integration of European Financial Markets, by David Folkerts-Landau and Donald J. Mathieson. 1989.
65. Managing Financial Risks in Indebted Developing Countries, by Donald J. Mathieson, David Folkerts-Landau, Timothy Lane, and Iqbal Zaidi. 1989.
64. The Federal Republic of Germany: Adjustment in a Surplus Country, by Leslie Lipschitz, Jeroen Kremers, Thomas Mayer, and Donogh McDonald. 1989.
63. Issues and Developments in International Trade Policy, by Margaret Kelly, Naheed Kirmani, Miranda Xafa, Clemens Boonekamp, and Peter Winglee. 1988.
62. The Common Agricultural Policy of the European Community: Principles and Consequences, by Julius Rosenblatt, Thomas Mayer, Kasper Bartholdy, Dimitrios Demekas, Sanjeev Gupta, and Leslie Lipschitz. 1988.
61. Policy Coordination in the European Monetary System. Part I: The European Monetary System: A Balance Between Rules and Discretion, by Manuel Guitián. Part II: Monetary Coordination Within the European Monetary System: Is There a Rule? by Massimo Russo and Giuseppe Tullio. 1988.
60. Policies for Developing Forward Foreign Exchange Markets, by Peter J. Quirk, Graham Hacche, Viktor Schoofs, and Lothar Weniger. 1988.

Note: For information on the title and availability of Occasional Papers not listed, please consult the IMF *Publications Catalog* or contact IMF Publication Services.